Gracefully
Broken yet
Restored

Tina Pullum

PAGE PUBLISHING, INC.
Conneaut Lake, PA

First originally published by Page Publishing 2021

ISBN 978-1-6624-3500-3 (pbk)
ISBN 978-1-6624-3501-0 (digital)

Printed in the United States of America

Contents

Foreword

SISTERHOOD IS LIKE silk. It's delicate and fragile, a secret bond that can't be broken. Tina's life will take you on a journey of both highs and lows, covered with grace and mercy. Her faith in God has become her cornerstone to lean on. Sisters, not in-laws, describes our relationship.

Our adventures are numerous and memorable, to say the least.

She's my Thelma. I'm her Louise. To know Tina is to love her. She has a pure love for women that is evident in her actions. Tina is a life seeker and a love giver. Overcoming life's challenges is her theme song.

Giving of herself is a calling and passion.

LaTanya Freeman

Acknowledgments

I WOULD LIKE to thank my children, Marques and Tiondda, for being the reason my heart beats. I've loved you with every fiber of my being and tried to make sure that I also lived a life of Christ before you. I have not always made the right decisions, but you still loved me in my shortcomings. You have supported me in every endeavor that I embarked upon, and I am grateful and thankful for the love that you both have given me in return. And from the two of you, I gained a daughter-in-love, Yessenia, along with my two beautiful grandchildren, Sa'riah and Tyrell.

I would like to thank my mother, Helen, and all my four siblings, Delandria, Darren, Shawn, and Shanon, for supporting me from day one until now. Whenever I needed you guys, you were always there for all my events or whatever. You had my back, and you loved me and loved me to be your daughter and older sister. Thanks for loving a sister the way you do.

I would like to thank my father- and mother-in-love, Leroy and Betty Pullum, for being the second parents in my life for thirty-eight years. You loved me, prayed for me, and supported everything I have achieved.

I would like to thank my brother- and sister-in-love, Harvey and LaTanya Freeman, for just being who you are in my life. Since I was the oldest of five, you became my older brother and sister. I thank you for the love, the support, the prayers, the travels, the laughs, and tears over the last thirty-eight years. Thank you for loving a sister the way you do.

I would like to acknowledge my spiritual parents, Dr. Fred and Linda Hodge of Living Praise Christian Center. I thank you for consistently living the life and allowing your steps to be ordered. Thank you for the word that you teach and show evidence in your own lives that I am what God says that I am and I can do what God says I can do and I can have absolutely everything that God said I could have. I thank you for your prayers, for your love, and for our sessions that we've had together. Thank you for encouraging me to keep dreaming.

I can't miss the opportunity to acknowledge my niece Shelly for taking out the time to help me bring my pages to life. You have supported me throughout the years in every which way, and you have stepped to the front and center. I am forever grateful for the love that you shed my way. You know how I feel about you and the bond we have. I say *thank you*. To your hubby, Ravanna, thank you for allowing your wife to take time from you in the evening and on weekends to help me bring this journey to manifestation on paper. Again, I love and thank you both.

Chapter 1

Gracefully Broken yet Restored

bro·ken
/'brōkən/
verb

1. past participle of break
adjective
2. having been fractured or damaged and no longer in one piece
synonyms
smashed, shattered, burst, fragmented, splintered, shivered, crushed, snapped, rent, torn, ruptured, separated, severed, in bits, in pieces, destroyed, wrecked, demolished, disintegrated, cracked, split, chipped, informal, fractured, damaged, injured, maimed
antonyms
whole, unbroken
3. (of a person) having given up all hope; despairing
synonyms
defeated, beaten, vanquished, overpowered, overwhelmed, subdued, demoralized, dispirited, dis-

couraged, dejected, crushed, humbled, dishon-
ored, ruined, crippled
re·store
/rəˈstôr/
verb
4. bring back (a previous right, practice, custom, or
   situation); reinstate
   synonyms
   reinstate, put back, replace, bring back, reinsti-
   tute, reimpose, reinstall, rehabilitate, reestablish,
   return to a former position/state
   antonyms
   abolish

IN JAPAN, THERE is an ancient practice called Kintsugi, an age-old custom where they make art by restoring broken things. The art of Kintsugi heals broken and cracked pottery by repairing it with powdered gold.

The Kintsugi custom is to repair a part of the old history of the object, with the understanding that the piece is more beautiful for having been broken. The style embraces the flaws and imperfections of the artifacts as well as highlights them.

For me, being gracefully broken means surrendering everything, pouring out your heart, and laying it at the feet of Jesus. Yet, I realize that He is more than capable of putting the pieces back together again—how He sees fit.

Sometimes, broken little girls and boys become wounded women and men. The pieces of life have been shattered within us. We should yet learn to allow God to draw us nearer to Him. He wants to be closer to us, even while we are in our brokenness. If we just endure and yield to His breaking process, it would be easier on us—much easier than if God were to break us against our will. God breaks us in order to remake us into what He wants us to be. He draws near to comfort us while we are being broken. Through the breaking and/or remaking process, God promises to give us a new heart.

Life's mishaps, dysfunctions in relationships, and unforeseen circumstances can sometimes break us—oftentimes severing our emotions. But thank God, after your pieces have been shattered, there is always a restoration that comes.

It is through His love that our brokenness becomes renewed like lacquered with gold.

Even after we try to collect and sweep up all the shattered pieces, only God can fully put us back together again.

Never be ashamed of the scars from your past or the broken places in your life. By highlighting our scars and brokenness with the beauty of strength, we thereby turn each and every crevice of pain into a golden pathway for life's journey. God breaks through all the mess. We are never beyond being healed and restored.

God is the potter, and we are His vessels. He is the one that repairs. This is where His craftsmanship comes into place. He can fit together the broken pieces that no longer seem to fit, transforming you right into a renewed and perfected creation. He works behind the scenes, mending, fitting together, and creating a better master-piece. He makes all things beautiful. Allow yourself to be put together with lacquered gold embroidered by love. Broken things can become blessed things if you let God do the mending.

I found myself with fragments and pieces that seemed to have been shattered from a place that there was no way I could be restored. Surely, even if I was restored, what use would it serve? Well, I can truly say that as of today, when I look back over my life, the paths and the roads, the things I have gone through, and the things that I have had to endure, I walk through my wilderness victorious.

To be restored, I had to use this understanding as a tool to min-ister to someone else, not realizing that it is used throughout the ministry. You should encourage someone else that is walking through bondage, a form of brokenness. Sometimes, we walk through life, and things happen that are out of our control, and we are not really sure how things will end up. I am in a place that I never thought I would be. God knew! He already has a plan, and He has a purpose for me. We don't know our journey or which path we are destined to take. I never really understood when people would say, "God will use your pain and your yesterday as a stepping-stone." I never really understood when people would say, "What you are going through is not just for you."

Right now, I am in a place where I have said, "How did I get from A to B and from C to D?" How did I do that? God knew! He knows the road I will have to take. He has a plan. He knows what has been prepared. He knows exactly what will be needed in order to get me through where I am, even today.

All I knew was to tell people the places I have been, letting them know the things that I have done in order to remove myself from the places that I was. Now today, I am yet restored, yet refined, yet refreshed. I have been rewound, and I am ready to restart. I don't look like, nor do I act like what I have been through. All things have worked together for my good. In other words, I have gone through the fire, but I don't have to smell like smoke.

I am somebody! I am here on purpose. There is nothing or no person that can stop what God has started. I am confident in this, "He that has begun a good work in me will complete it!" So now I can look back. When I said, "How did I get from A to B and from C to D?" How did I do that? God knew!

Until you're broken, you don't know what you're made of. It gives you the ability to build yourself all over again but stronger than before. I learned that you never know how strong you are until being strong is the only choice you have. So I sit today as a woman that was gracefully broken, and I say gracefully because the pieces were put back together again and restored. My relationship and foundation were shaken. But they were never removed. I sit at a place now where I am contented. I am happy! I have peace within me, a kind of peace that the world couldn't give me, so the world can't take it away.

In my studies, I have meditated on the following:

> Being confident of this very thing, that He which hath begun a good work in you will per-form it until the day of Jesus Christ. (Philippians 1:6)

Behold, I am making all things new. (Revelation 21:5)

Therefore, if anyone is in Christ, he is a new creation. The old has passed away, behold, the new has come. (2 Corinthians 5:17)

He heals the brokenhearted and binds up their wounds. (Psalm 147:3)

He made everything beautiful in its time. (Ecclesiastes 3:11)

Chapter 2

I Overcame, I Conquered, and I Exhaled

I OVERCAME, I conquered, and I exhaled! I overcame the obstacles, the trials, the tribulations, the downfalls, the pitfalls, the mishaps, the disappointments, the hurt, the pain, the confusion, and the loss. I was overcome by the blood of the Lamb. I couldn't have done this without God. I conquered everything that was released from the pit of hell that seemed to be personally assigned to me. A hellish torment was attacking my mind, tormenting my soul, a torment that penetrated every fiber of my being.

Greater is He that is in me than He that is in the world. And they must have forgotten that God told me that no weapon in any form, shape, or fashion would prosper against me. Oh yeah, they formed, but because I overcame them, they could not continue to prosper in my life, hindering my purpose and my destiny—my destiny that has already been laid out way before they were ever formed.

I am more than a conqueror. I'm at a place of peace. I was released and freed from everything that I overcame and everything that I had to conquer. I am at a place where now I can breathe. While I'm breathing, I can exhale because the joy of the Lord is my strength. I have learned to exhale every negative experience and every trauma and inhale His presence, His peace, and His love.

He has given me so much peace, the kind of peace which surpasses all understanding. This has guarded my heart. As you read my journey, you will see, there was a time that I did not smile. Now I have a reason to smile. He has given me a reason to laugh and a reason to "dance like nobody's watching!" He has given me a reason to continue to have faith in Him and His promises each and every day.

While looking back on yesterday, looking back at all the stepping-stones upon which I had to embark, today, I can truly say that this was the path best traveled. This path was how I got to where I am now. Each step that I took made me stronger. Each step that I accepted and embraced rooted me, allowing me to go to a deeper level. It helped me to embrace and withstand the storm.

My sister gave me a blanket that said, they whispered to her, "You cannot withstand the *storm*." She whispered back, *"I am the storm."* I can truly attest to that. I have been through some storms along my life's journey. I've learned in life to overcome and to conquer the good with the bad, unfortunately, at times, even the ugly. Instead of living in the shadow of yesterday though, I walk in the light of today and the hope of tomorrow. I stand firm on the foundation that quitting is *not* an option, and because, by nature, I am a fighter, I don't quit easily. I don't fight for victory. I fight from victory. I am more than a conqueror.

I'll never be who I was again, I'll never be what I was again, and I'll never see things the way I used to see them again. I'm better now. I didn't just survive what happened. I'm better because of what happened. I know that I am not defined by my past, my faults, nor my failures. God planted a seed within me. No matter what the world throws at me, I have the strength to rise above. I am much stronger than that, that, and even that. This is why today, I will say, "I overcame, I conquered, and now I can exhale."

Chapter 3

The First but Treated the Worst

I WAS THE first child. I was the first grandchild, and I was born the first niece on my dad's side of the family. Born in Oklahoma, my parents were very young. They were sixteen and seventeen years of age. My parents got married before I was born, but they never lived together. They were both in high school, seniors at that time. I became like a mascot for the Douglas High School class of 1960. I was the baby born that year, so I grew up with them.

As time went by, my dad was incarcerated for petty theft. He went to jail for stealing from a store. While he was in jail, my mom, of course, needed some assistance with the basic necessities, such as diapers and milk. My mom would always tell me stories about my grandfather. Apparently, he would always say that if we ever needed something to eat, that dinner would be ready by a certain time. This was his way of helping out, I guess since his son could offer no familial support from behind bars.

While dad was in jail, my mom filed for divorce. I was still a little girl. I do remember that my dad did come to visit when he got out. I must have been no more than four or five years old. I remember it like it was yesterday. He brought me an orange and a white fur coat. He bent down to give me this coat. He was so happy about it too. I remember it clearly. I took the coat and walked over to the wall heater. I tried to burn that coat. As I think about it, it is really sad that I was so young. Still, I was harboring so much anger toward him. I can recall not wanting to have anything to do with him or that coat. As time moved forward, I would see him from time to time, here and there throughout the years. It seems it was more there than here actually. Overall, I remember all the broken promises. He was going to buy me school clothes, or he was going to do this, and he often promised to do that.

My grandmother soon became a liaison between us. Sometimes, I needed things as a young girl coming up. When I needed things, I would call my grandmother. She would say, "Let me ask your dad." That was always her response. That drove me crazy. First of all, she knew he wasn't doing anything for me. So every time I asked, I would find myself thinking, *What does he have to do with this?* Then I would scream within myself, of course, thinking, *This is your money!* But nevertheless, of course, she, too, never came through. Keep in mind, I was the oldest grandchild. All the other grandchildren on my dad's side of the family always seemed to be at grandmother's house. From my perspective, compared to them, I felt the difference in how I was treated. They were fed with a silver spoon, if you ask me.

My grandfather owned some apartment buildings in Oklahoma. As I got older, we lived there. They were likely for people that were of lower income. During those times, my dad would come over to the apartments but not to see me. He was in the area to see the mother of one of my friends. They were dating at the time. Without fail, every time he would come to visit them, he would take them gifts. Of course, my friend couldn't wait to come and rub it in my face. I would always say, in a sassy but defensive tone, "I don't care!" Deep down, I did care.

The resentment eventually would rise up. The anger I felt and my hatred toward him began to build up more and more. I couldn't help reminiscing and remembering all the broken promises, remembering that he would never come through on things—not at all a man of his word. There was a thorn in my side. I knew that all the other grandkids were being spoiled, and nobody really cared about me. I felt that I was kicked to the curb. I was the oldest, the firstborn baby girl. I didn't understand why I was rejected by him and my grandparents.

I remember one of my great aunts would always try to instill in me that I shouldn't hate my dad. Meanwhile, he was always telling people that my family was teaching me to dislike him. Little did he know, it was the exact opposite. They were trying to teach me to love him. I remember one day, I was in the ninth grade, and I was staying at my aunt's house. He was supposedly coming over to take me shopping for school. I didn't trust him. In those days, I used to carry a little Indian pocketknife. I told myself, "I'm going to take this knife just in case because I don't trust it! If I need it, I will use it."

The funny thing about it, one of my cousins, as I was getting ready to leave, she said, "Make sure you take something with you." We knew that I knew that she meant a weapon because she knew I was going to spend the day with my dad. We knew that we couldn't trust him. We knew I needed to protect myself. The thought of it, it's so sad that a girl going on a shopping trip with her daddy is carrying a little Indian pocketknife to protect herself.

As time went on and the years passed, we drifted further apart. I grew to despise the ground that he walked on. I had so much anger and so much bitterness toward him. It was during this time that I was living in California. He was still in Oklahoma. He had remarried, and she had two children. I was in high school. I remember him being diabetic, so he received social security benefits. He was already receiving other supplementary benefits too. When he remarried, however, he had my benefits cut down to $47 a month. The benefits that he received had been split between her kids and me. Mind you, her kids were living with them. He was already taking care of them. They were a family.

As I got older, a few times, I tried—I tried to "go high, and he would always go low." Even though that was my reality with him, I did the right thing. I made an effort to reach out. I called him. Before it was all said and done, before it was over, over, something happened. He ended up mad and hung up the phone.

So here I am, a young lady to be with my own family, a life lived without him, and all I ever wanted was the love from my daddy.

Because of him, I didn't experience growing up with my grandparents. We were all right in the same state, no more than maybe thirty minutes away until I moved. I never grew up with stories of people in my family, like the ones telling stories about going to their grandma's house. I went to my grandmother's house a few times, here and there. I could probably count those times on one hand.

Subsequently, when I was younger, I would always say, "If something happens to my dad, I don't wanna go to the funeral." I would always say, "God, if something happens?" I did not want to go to his funeral. I didn't want to be a hypocrite either. We did not have a healthy relationship. He didn't care for me, and I didn't care for him. I did not want to go to his funeral. It seems harsh for a child to say that about their dad, but this is how he made me feel. I was so adamant. Repeatedly, I said that as a young child. That was one thing I knew I wasn't doing.

Now years have passed, and I remember it clearly. My husband and I were preparing for a trip to Tahiti. It was the day before we were getting ready to leave. We were anticipating the moment we would be able to enjoy the land of paradise. I got a phone call that night. It was one of my aunts, my dad's sister. She was calling to let me know that my dad had died.

He was a diabetic. It was said that it might have been complications from pneumonia. They were letting me know that they were getting ready to have the funeral. He had already died the week before. I stood tall when I inhaled and proudly exhaled while telling her that I was on my way out of the country, and I could not attend the funeral. As far back as I could remember, I was always telling God I did not want to go to his funeral. And it happened at a time that I could not go. So I hung up the phone. Wouldn't you know it, it messed me up. I was now mad and angry because he died two days before my birthday. Now I would have to forever remember when he died.

When I look back on that now, I was really still locked up in bondage. Man, oh man, oh man. But that's how I felt, as crazy as it sounds. I remembered how one of my friends, Addie, told me, "Tina, you need to forgive your father, and you need to forgive yourself in order to let it go."

I said, "He's already dead!"

She said, "But you still need to ask him for forgiveness, not for him, for you!" She said that in order for me to forgive myself. She told me to order some flowers to send to the funeral home or to the house.

I was like, "What?"

She said, "Yes! I need you to order some flowers."

So I left work and went to the local florist. I was so mad when I got there. I went in with an attitude. I stomped to the counter, pouting internally, and I told the girl that I need to order some flowers.

She asked me how much I wanted to spend and what the occasion was. I said my dad died, and I was told to send him some flowers. I guess the way that I said that she was taken aback. She looked very surprised by my response. I proceeded with my order by giving her my address. She wanted an additional address for the delivery, and I told her that if no one was home to just leave the flowers, leave them on the back porch. I didn't really care. She looked up at me, surprised. It must have been my tone and the way that I responded. I told her, "I am so sorry! This is the hardest thing that I've ever had to do." I told her how my dad and I did not get along and how much I did not care for him. I further explained to this stranger how my friend told me I needed to order flowers in order to ask him for forgiveness. I told her I needed to do this in order for me to move forward.

So the young girl that was behind the counter said, "Okay, I understand." But deep down, I couldn't help but think, *I don't think she really understood because she still has this look of shock on her face.* I walked out of the florist to my car. I called my friend Addie. I said, "I did what you told me to do, and now I am done!"

We finally arrived in Tahiti. We had reserved the most beautiful bungalow. The wall that was directly in front of the bed was made out of glass. The ocean, yes, the ocean, was about 10 feet away from my balcony. There was an outdoor shower. The ambiance in the bungalow, the view from my balcony caused a sensory overload. It was so beautiful and breathtaking I cried. It looked like it was something right out of a magazine. Mind you, I had been on an emotional roller coaster for the last few days, so my crazy self and I was still mad. I was mad about my dad dying right before my birthday. Lord, please help me.

That night, I remember my husband, Clifton, told me that I needed to let it go. He reminded me again, just like Addie, that I needed to forgive him and let go. He told me that he felt my dad was upset that I had made it without him in spite of his lack, his deficient contributions, how he underprovided financially, his lack of concern for not playing a major part in my life. Well, I succeeded without him.

My dad was a controlling person. He was used to controlling people, but he could not control me. Clifton also said, "You need to release this and let it go now. We are in paradise. Why are you holding on to this anger and bitterness in the midst of paradise?"

At the moment, I asked my father for forgiveness, and I asked myself for forgiveness, and I let it go. The next morning, I woke up in paradise. I had let go of all the residue, the strongholds that I had brought with me to Tahiti, emotional luggage that had me bound. We enjoyed the rest of our trip in paradise. To this day, I no longer allow that residue to disrupt my life again.

As I said in the beginning, I was the first child. I was the first grandchild, and I was born the first niece on my dad's side of the family. All my other cousins, they were fed with a silver spoon if you had asked me. I might have been the only one that grew beyond my circumstances. I continued to walk with God. My grandfather was the pastor of a Nazarene church. When he died, my father took it over. Now when I look back, I am humbled. To this day, some of my cousins are alcoholics, some are on drugs, and some have been in and out of jail. I even heard that I was a prostitute for a minute.

They were fed with a silver spoon if you had asked me. The truth was everything. The scriptures said, "The last shall be first and the first shall be last." I think that's exactly what happened. Right now, today, my walk with God is stronger than ever before. I no longer think or feel that I was treated as the worst. Right now, I feel loved and cherished. I finally know that to my heavenly Father, I am His daughter being treated as His first. There is no love like the love I receive from God.

Chapter 4

Hide-and-Seek

YOU ARE PROBABLY wondering why I am calling this chapter hide-and-seek. This is about the season of my life that I find myself hiding from my violator. I was hiding myself from those that were seeking, lurking, and prowling. They were after my innocence. Growing up as a little girl, I can't even tell you, I don't even know how many times I was violated by my seeker.

I remember one family member would use his sister for the hunt. He would have her entice me with hopes of fun and little girl giggles. She would ask me to come over to their house to play. We lived on the same street, so getting me there was the easy part. I was summoned often. I would come over to play, and it never failed. She would leave. Apparently, he was giving her money so that she would leave and go down the street to the local candy store. While she was gone, joyfully headed to the local candy store, he would begin the game. He would seek me out joyfully as if he, too, were headed to the local candy store. I was afraid. I was fearful and really didn't understand. I knew that it wasn't right. Back in those days, nobody ever talked about somebody touching you inappropriately because our parents were never taught to have that conversation.

My seeker was so bold and persistent in seeking me out. Sometimes, when we would leave church, the car would be full of family members. That didn't stop him. We didn't wear seat belts back then. In those days, you would easily fit a lot of people in the car. We rode with about ten people deep on occasion.

My seeker would always grab me up and make me sit right on his lap. And I would be stuck, nowhere to go, no words that I could say. So I would sit right on his lap. I will never forget. I can never forget how he would put two fingers in his mouth. The other fingers from his other hand would be up under my dress, inside of me, right on his lap. I was too afraid. I didn't even know what to say. I didn't know how to say. I was too afraid. There were people right there. We rode with about ten people deep on occasion. I was so afraid. My seeker would always grab me up and make me sit, right on his lap. It put me in a place of not understanding. Don't they see it? But I knew. I knew that it was just not right. I was hiding right there in broad daylight, and my seeker was still able to find me. My seeker would always grab me up and make me sit right on his lap.

But oh, it didn't stop there. I had another close family member that was babysitting my siblings and me one night. I was woken up from a deep sleep, and there he was, lying on top of me. He put his hands over my mouth. Again, I tried to hide within to make myself small and invisible. But I knew. I knew that it was just not right. I never said anything about that either. I knew that my seeker would always find me. I didn't quite know how to tell somebody that he touched me inappropriately. So here I was again.

Time moved on. I had a third seeker that found me. He was much older than the other two. He was a close friend of the family, and he was babysitting my siblings and me one night. This time, I found myself asleep, and again, I woke up to my seeker finding me. Again, I never said anything. By now, I was living in shock, traumatized. I woke up to my seeker finding me. Here we are again and again and again, the nightmare again! What do I do? Who's going to believe me? What do I say? I wish I am invisible. I'm scared. I don't understand.

Back then, back in those days, I was a quiet, shy, innocent little girl. I just tried to abide by the rules and be a good listener. I did what I was told. So all this time, my seekers were taking advantage of me.

Not only was I trying to hide from them, but I was trying to hide from the inside. I needed to be invisible. In those times, that took me to hell and back. I was essentially walking around with all that hurt. Youthful confusion, strongholds, and brokenness, they were all going on inside. It felt like darkness inside that would eventually overcome me, a void that taunted me. And I carried it for years.

It wasn't until later on that I found out that one of my seekers had found some other relatives to seek. They, too, were afraid, hiding in closets and making themselves small. They, too, wanted to be invisible. Yet they were still found. When this relative and I started exchanging the details of our stories, it was years later. It was already too late to press charges because over twenty years had already passed. The statute of limitations had expired.

After hearing her truth, I was finally freed and able to talk about it. I cried out and asked God to help me get rid of all that I had been carrying. I told Him I was tired of hiding from the inside out. I was tired of carrying this void, this darkness around with me. I was tired of hiding from myself. When I would see things on television about people being molested, all that he did to me would cause havoc inside of me. It was like all that I had bottled up and suppressed would stir around in my mind in a burst of horrific feelings and emotions. I couldn't hide it anymore.

Life moved on. Now I am a young girl trying to be who I am supposed to be and still growing up in the church. I knew that my love for God was my foundation. In spite of what had happened to me, I was chosen.

Our church had a youth pastor who was married to his beautifully pregnant wife. His wife was in the hospital having a C-section performed to bring into this world their first child. Little did I know what was to come. To my surprise, another seeker found me. He took advantage of me like the others. I didn't know what to do. I was afraid to say anything. How could I when his wife was in the hospital having a C-Section performed to bring into this world their first child? I didn't want his trespass of my innocence to hurt her. I didn't want to hurt the family. I didn't want to hurt those that would have been involved from the church. Needless to say, he had no remorse nor a repentant heart. He was a predator. He became comfortable and cocky. One day, he had the audacity to tell me, "I've had you before your future husband has even had you." Oh, how he taunted me. Now that was a hard pill to swallow. That, too, I would carry with me. I added it right to my luggage.

My first three seekers violated and molested me. We were living in Oklahoma. Now we were living in California. This last seeker, I saw him often because our families were close. We lived in the same area, and we went to the same church. So that means, every week, I had to suffer in silence. I had to deal with this stronghold alone. I just wanted to be invisible.

I had another seeker that was not successful. I was about seventeen years old. I don't recall why, but for some reason, I was home and not at school. I was running the vacuum cleaner but still in my pajamas. One of my brothers had stayed home from school that day. He was about thirteen. Sometimes, he would be defiant and refuse to go to school. In those days, it wasn't odd or rare to leave the doors of your home unlocked. It was daytime, which meant we were safe. As I was vacuuming and my brother was lying on the couch, the front door to our apartment opened. A man walked in, wearing a ski mask. I turned to look at him. I was startled, but I shouted, "Get out of here!" At that same moment, my brother simultaneously raised up from the couch, spewing a few choice words. We lived in Oklahoma. He was thirteen. Clearly, the man wasn't ready to tussle, so he slowly backed up to the door and left our apartment.

My brother asked me who it was. For some reason, I had a feeling that I knew who it was. I knew it was the man from upstairs. His name was Franklin. My brother jumped up off of the couch as if it was on fire and sprinted up those stairs two at a time to give him a few more choice words. Franklin was suddenly faced with the scowl and pulsing anger of my adolescent brother, the fearless protector of our home. Franklin stuttered and attempted to say, "Oh, I, I was just playing. Did I scare you guys?"

Well, I didn't know it back then, but later in life, my brother told me that Franklin, the following year, went to jail. He was incarcerated for raping a couple of young girls in the neighborhood. So in hindsight, if my brother had not been home from school that day, Franklin might have been coming down to rape me. When that reality hit me, my mind went to the Word of God. I cried out, "Lord! I thank you for keeping me from danger, seen and not seen."

From all the deeply rooted hiding that I had endured, once again, I was tormented to the core of my very soul. Now what was I supposed to do? I hid from the others that hunted me. I hid. I took all that I was feeling, memorializing every infringement, and I hid. I suppressed it as much as I could. I had to dig deep to cover up the silent shame.

Now this. I must take this violation and hide it too. Wow! Enough is enough! How much can I hide? How long do I have to carry all this around?

I got to a place where all I could say was "I can't do this anymore!" I cried out to God and said, "I need you! It's too dark in here! I need some light! Please help me!" And He did just that. He came in, and He reminded me who I was. He reminded me how much He loved me. He reminded me that I was fearfully and wonderfully made. That's what He did for me.

So I opened up from all the hiding that was going on, even when I was afraid, and I didn't know how to openly express it. How do you share this private turmoil? I knew I wasn't going to allow this anymore. I told my Father, "God, I am going to hold your hand, and I am going to trust you. I need you, Lord, to walk me through this." He did it. He answered my prayers. I got stronger.

Well, tell someone I did. I got to a place where I was able to tell my husband after we got married. I told him everything that happened to me when I was younger. I shared with my mother the struggles that I had endured. She, of course, was devastated. As a parent, you want to protect your child. But how could she protect me when I didn't know how to tell her what was happening. I told my children what happened too. Then God ordered my steps and used me as a vessel. He put me in places in front of people, doing and saying things that I would never have imagined having the strength to say. I started ministering to other women about being molested and taken advantage of. I shared my story. I witnessed to all who would hear. I shared my truth of how I was suffering in silence, trying to hide from my seeker.

So today, I look back, and I am stronger, and I am wiser. They were after my innocence. I know that I no longer have to hide myself from those that were seeking, lurking, and prowling. Because what the enemy meant for evil, God turned it around for my good. I have been able to reach back and share my story and help somebody else to come out from hiding. We've all played the game as a child, hide-and-seek, and yet the enemy will use anyone. Sometimes, the seeker is someone that is close to you. They are hunters, and they often seek and take advantage of the innocent. They seek to destroy you. Even the ones that are the closest to you can be the hunter. They seek to fulfill their own selfish lust. We call it a game. But sometimes, it winds up being more than just a game because you find yourself in a position that while they are seeking, you are constantly trying to hide.

Chapter 5

Born a Fighter, from Physical to Spiritual

IN THIS PARTICULAR chapter, my brother suggested since everything else he felt was showing my weakness and not my strengths. He reminded me that he felt that I was the strongest person that he knew. I needed to let people know that I was born a fighter, a fighter born to survive obstacles, trials, and tribulations. After all the things that I had endured, I was ready to take on anything that was headed my way.

When I was younger, I fought with my fist. I had so many fights with my boy cousins. One of my brothers was nonstop worrisome. He tried my patience as a hobby. As I think about it now, most of my fights were with boys. So I'm going to tell you about a couple of rounds that had them second-guessing themselves about little bitty me. I reminded people regularly that I just look like this.

Round 1: *Ding!*

I had a fight with a boy named Reggie that lived in the same apartment complex as my family and me. We were living in Dungee, Oklahoma. I don't know how old we were, probably in elementary school, about the fourth or fifth grade. Back in the day, there were instigators within the crowd that would be a little extra. They would come and put sticks on your shoulders so that it could be knocked off. This is exactly what happened one day when Reggie wanted to be a tough guy. I was in one corner, and he was in the other. There was a crowd that circled around us. The spectators were anxious, gesturing, and yelling out phrases that they had practiced for a time such as this. We were inside a Laundromat of all places.

I was clearly feeling confident because my chest poked out slightly as I stood still for the instigator to put the stick on my shoulder. He was being dramatic as if he needed to put it in just the right spot. Meanwhile, Reggie was standing there, holding on to his piece of a branch. Somebody from the other crew pushed him. His stick hit the side of my face, barely missing my right eye. Had I flinched, there would have been a different version of events. Now what did they do that for? I went from zero to a hundred real quick. I took that stick, and I tried to beat him down. I was trying to finish him. I beat him so bad he ran and jumped into one of the Laundromat dryers, trying to escape my wrath. I accommodated him by slamming the door of the dryer, then I walked off. The crowd roared with excitement, slapping fives and cackling harder than necessary.

I won that round, but I still have the scar on my face to this today. It has faded a lot over the years. But it is a forever reminder of that first-round win.

Round 2: *Ding!*

Again, here we were, still in Dungee, Oklahoma. We were living in the same apartment complex. Now I was probably in the sixth or seventh grade. I know I was in junior high school. I remember specifically how we were bused to the other side of town, otherwise known as the "other side of the railroad tracks." They called it integration. We were brought up in the church, and there were certain understandings. We couldn't just spend the night at our friend's homes, so we didn't even ask because some of the kids would be smoking or drinking. Actually, we were not allowed to go to their house pretty much at all, especially if their mother wasn't home. This girl from my school named Yolana lived in the neighborhood a couple of blocks away. She lived in a house with her mother, father, and older siblings. They would smoke and drink at their house. Their house was a popular spot because they would play music, dance, and have parties.

That illicit home was engaging in secular things that were in total contradiction to our sheltered world as church kids.

One day, I don't know exactly how it happened. Some way or another, we were on the bus, and something happened. Yolana and I didn't really know each other, but we were supposed to have a fight that day after school. Now ask me why and what we were going to be fighting over, I don't even remember. All I know is I was in the ring for the second time. I kept a little object available for my protection, as needed if needed. It wasn't uncommon for someone back in the day to have a secret weapon. Well, this chick pulled "the secret weapon" out on me. She had one of those acrylic finger rings. I had no idea. We got off the bus and began to fight. That girl hit me in my eye with that ring. I saw stars just like the ones I had seen on a cartoon I had watched on TV before.

After I gathered myself, I wisely decided the round was over for me. I headed straight home. My eye had turned black-and-blue just that fast. Along with it being discolored and painful, it had swollen to the size of a golf ball. It began to pulsate. I looked in the side mirror of a car. Until I looked in the mirror, I hadn't realized that I couldn't see out of it.

I had never been in such excruciating pain. I had never seen a black eye in real life, only on TV. When I got home, we put some ice on it. In my pretend thoughts, I wanted to put a steak on it like I had seen on TV. Because I lived on the lower-income side of steak ownership, the ice it was. I finally got to, I mean had to, stay home from school for a day. I didn't know what I was going to do. I was devastated that I literally had a black eye. That fight with Yolana was my first fight with a girl. All my other fights had been with boys. Although our worlds were so different, she and I became the best of friends. It was the strangest thing.

She was so lucky. I yearned to be in the world that she lived in, and I think she was attracted to my world too. My mom came home after work every day. We had the typical little Christian family home, unlike her. Her mom and dad were gone most of the time, and she was always with her older siblings. Usually, she was pretty much on her own. After the dust between us settled, I began to recognize that we both desired to "trade places." We became the best of friends. And for the record, yes, I lost round 2. *Ding!*

Round 3: *Ding!*

We were still living in Oklahoma. It was a common occurrence for me to fight with my one brother, one more than the other. My cousins and I regularly tousled.

One of my cousins, in particular, I'm going to call him Jimmy. That boy was always bothering me. He liked to play jokes on people all the time. I was the type that if I could not get to you with my hands because you are holding me down, I would bite you. I couldn't stand to be held down. So if I couldn't do anything else, I was going to bite you, not just a nibble like a warning bite. I was going to bite what I called a plug out of you—down to your, as they say, "White meat." I was for sure going to leave my brand. Definitely, I was intentionally leaving a substantial mark. I'd left a few of my teeth marks on that boy, along with my brother and other boy cousins. I am not sure if I won that round but *ding!*

Round 4: *Ding!*

I was an eighth grader in Carson, California. We walked home from school every day. We were in junior high school. Valerie, my friend, was in the seventh grade. Our families were very close. Our mothers knew each other when we used to live in Oklahoma before both families moved to California. Not only did we go to the same school, but also we went to the same church. We would sometimes hang out at her house since they had a swimming pool. Valerie, that silly girl, she liked to play all the time. One day, we were walking home, and she hit me in the back of my head with her fist. Then she would just take off running ahead. She would be just laughing like it was the funniest thing. She would be so tickled. I was still a quiet and shy kind of girl. So being low-key and not overly emotional, I would say, "Valerie, don't do that again." She would just laugh it off like there was nothing to it. Of course, everyone around us would laugh right along with her, at my expense. On another day, she did it for a second time. As before, she again was tickled as she ran off laughing. I found myself repeating myself and telling her again. Trust me, I was trying to warn her.

I said, "Valerie, don't hit me again, and I am not playing with you!" Here we were on a different day. School had dismissed, and we were walking our usual path home. Here came Valerie. She socked me in my back. This would be the third and last time that she put her hands on me. Again, she just laughed.

As they said, "Three strikes, you're out!" I zoned out, and everything went dark.

Before I knew it, I snatched her up off of her feet and slammed her down to the ground. When I came to myself, I had my knee in her neck. I told her, "As long as you live, don't you ever put your hands on me again!" Valerie was not a handsome girl. She had big eyes. I'm not sure, but her bulging eyes said thyroid problem. Anyway, her eyes were about to pop out of her head. All she could do was nod and agree. So she did. She nodded, and she agreed. All those that stood by were frozen in place. I slowly got up, and I backed away from the situation. She got up, and she gathered herself and her stuff. With this newfound understanding, we all continued to walk home, and that was the end of that round. That one was mine. *Ding!*

Round 5: *Ding!*

One of my brothers was always fighting with my sister. They went so many rounds that I lost track. Most of the time, if he was getting the best of her, I would jump in to help her. But this one particular time, they were fighting, and I jumped in as usual. When my brother was in the middle of swinging his fist back, he hit me so hard that I fell to the ground. Not only did it catch me by surprise, but it also caught him by surprise. He stopped in his tracks, realizing what had happened. He looked at his fist.

He was about thirteen or fourteen years old. It seemed he realized that he, too, was strong. We were suddenly evenly matched. He didn't have to be afraid of me, his big sister, anymore. After that knockdown that he just delivered on accident, I recall that was the last time that I jumped in to help my sister against my brother. She was officially going to have to fend for herself from there on. It was kind of like when Joe Fraiser knocked down the World Champion Muhammad Ali with that left hook. Needless to say, my brother won that round. *Ding!*

Round 6: *Ding!*

There was a boy in the neighborhood that was bothering one of my brothers. My brother came home and told me that this boy named Daniel from the neighborhood had taken something from him. I didn't remember the story until my brother brought it back to my memory recently. He said I had stormed out of the house, and I went down to that boy's house, and I let him know that he was not allowed. He was no longer allowed to look at, talk to, bully, bother, or do anything to my brother again. I told him if I found out anything different, I would come back and take care of him. And I made sure he understood the warning that I gave him. After that, my brother said that I had changed his whole life that day. I had confronted the bully, who no longer bullied him. He said he felt that I was the strongest person that he knew because I confronted his giant named Daniel. I guess I can say that I won that round for my brother. *Ding!*

Round 7: *Ding!*

I was in the eleventh grade, and I was going to Banning High, which is located in Wilmington, California. I was in my art class. Again, I still lived by the rule of three strikes and you are out. There was a boy in my class named Lawrence. He had a girlfriend, and she was in my gym class. She was kind of cute, I guess. On that particular day, I started not feeling well while I was in class. So I laid my head down on the table. It was a taller art table, so it was the perfect height. While I was trying to zone out, somebody hit me on the top of my head. I, of course, raised up my head, ready for action. I said, "Whoever did it, don't do it again." After I blared out this assertion, because I thought I had just spoken and made it clear that I didn't need to say anything else, so I slowly laid my head back down. Nevertheless, I got a second hit across the back of my head. That time, I immediately lifted my head up, and I said, "You know what, this is the last time. Whoever did it bet not do it again." We were about to go to the third strike, and I tried my best to warn whomever. This was about to happen. I knew I couldn't make any promises. Needless to say, I got a slap across the back of my head for the third time. I jumped up, and Lawrence was standing there. I pushed the table into him, I picked up the X-Acto knife that was on my table, and before I saw stars, I threw the knife at him.

It hit him in his face. It cut him under his eye, then it hit him on his arm before falling to the table. I pushed the table back, and I charged at him like he was wearing all red, and I was a bull straight from the bullring in Mexico. The teacher and some other students ran over and broke us up, but she screamed at me and said, "What are you doing? You could have seriously injured him. He has been cut. You both go to the office!" And I told her he wouldn't leave me alone. I warned him. I gave him three chances, and he didn't take the warning. So we both walked down to the principal's office. Both of us had to tell our side of the story. It didn't matter that he hit me. It didn't matter that I warned him three times. All that mattered to them was that I could have seriously injured him.

I got suspended for three days from school. I found out later that it was Lawrence that was hitting me on my head in my art class. I guess those were supposed to be love taps. One of his friends told me that Lawrence said he liked me, even though I knew he had a girl-friend. Wouldn't you think that by the eleventh grade, a boy would be able to say that he likes you? That would be a much better approach, definitely better than slapping me across my head. We used to ride the same bus to school, and after that, his father would drop him off at school every day and pick him up. I would still see his girlfriend in my gym class, but she kept her distance from me. That was the end of that round. *Ding!*

Round 8: *Ding!*

I was blossoming as a young woman in the city of Carson, California. I was probably about twenty-one. My boyfriend Clifton, who became my future husband, was over my house for a visit. Out of nowhere, my brother came rushing into the house, completely out of breath. Clifton and I were both startled and surprised to see him so emotional. He had just come from Mr. Cedric's house. He was the neighbor that lived across the street with his daughter. For whatever reason, Mr. Cedric said something crazy or did something to him. I don't know what happened that particular night, but I remembered I immediately charged out of the house and went directly across the street, heading toward Mr. Cedric's. I felt an intense heat inside, and my heart was beating fast. I felt like I was going to snap. All I knew is, I was going to beat this man down. I knew this old man could easily get the best of me and beat me like the child I was. He was old enough to be my father. I couldn't stand a trifling, disrespectful man. But I had snapped, and I was on my way across the street. I walked up to that old man to give him a piece of my mind or my two cents for sure. He was going to hear from me on this day. I was going to get him straightened right out! Immediately, before I could step up on the curb, Clifton grabbed me. Startled, I tried to snatch away, but he held on to me and began pulling me back. I felt his correction because he made me go into the house. Well, he locked me in the house. I was strongly advised, well, he suggested that I calm down. He told me, "You can't go over there and try to beat up that old man! What's wrong with you?" So I thought about it, and I began to feel embarrassed. Clifton hadn't seen this side of me before. In all honesty, that man could have beat me down. Wow! God's mercy. All I knew is that you better not mess with my sister or my brothers. My brothers and sisters and I didn't always get along, but no one else is going to mess with them, not on my watch. *Ding!*

As I got older, eventually, I learned to rechannel all that dark energy up to a certain point, at least. Well, let's just say I learned to control and manage my mandatory "three strikes, you're out" rule. People will test your patience all the time. To be honest, all that I had endured, my suppressed bondage in captivity, simply caused some things to lay dormant. But please don't wake this side of her up. I'm just saying. I'm getting too old to continue to fight with my fist.

Some time has passed since my last demand for respect. I have moved to Palmdale, California, and I joined a church. I wanted to be active, and I needed my steps to be ordered once again. I prayed to the Lord, and I became a part of the intercessory prayer group.

It was in that prayer training, well, boot camp, that we learned about spiritual warfare. I learned to fight with the word of the sword, the book of the gospel known as the Bible. In that boot camp, we learned how to recognize when you're in spiritual warfare. We read books like *He Came to Set the Captive Free, Dress to Kill, Dialog with*

God, and Free in Christ, to name a few. That's when I learned to fight with the Word of God. I learned how important it was to put on my armor going in for a battle. I learned to decree and declare. I learned to go boldly with confidence before the throne. We attended conferences with Cindy Trimm, prayer nights with Sarah Morgan, and other training that prepared us for a spiritual battle. I have learned to stand up and take my boxing gloves off. I have learned to stand on God's Word when I don't know what else to do. Oh, I sometimes struggled not to pick up the boxing gloves, but now I just pick up the Word of God and go before the throne while allowing him to fight my battles because He did tell me that vengeance was His.

In my studies, I have meditated on the following:

> Dearly beloved, do not avenge yourselves,
> but rather give place to wrath; for it is written,
> "Vengeance is mine, I will repay," says the Lord.
> (Roman 12:19)

And he said, Hearken ye, all Judah, and ye inhabitants of Jerusalem, and thou king, Jehoshaphat, Thus saith the Lord unto you, Be not afraid nor dismayed by reason of this great multitude; for the battle is not yours, but God's. (2 Chronicles 20:15)

Chapter 6

Russian Roulette and Pulling the Trigger

I WAS A young teenager. I'm not quite sure how old I was at this point in my life. I know I was at a place in my life that the heaviness of the molestations from my past, I buried but still carried the burden of its presence around with me constantly. The rejection from my father and his family was weighing heavy and suppressing me down even more. I was misunderstood. Everything that I tried to say, people misunderstood. Nobody understood. Well, that frustrated me even more. It seemed like no one could understand where I was coming from—probably because they didn't know all the hell that I was walking around with inside, so that frustrated me more.

I could be walking down the street or in the mall somewhere, and strangers would look at me and say, "Why don't you smile?" And man, oh man, that would send me to a place where I would be so mad and so angry. I was thinking, *Excuse me! You don't even know me, you don't know anything about me, you don't even know what has happened to me, and you're asking me to smile, for what?* That just made me even madder. I guess they could see a very young girl walking around with so much anger that it was displayed all over my face. I felt nobody could relate. I held everything in, and then I was not very vocal.

One afternoon, I was in my room, and my mind began to drift. The noise from the inside began to get louder and louder. The enemy got me to a place where it began to talk to me. It would whisper to me, calling my name. It cornered me, and I felt it isolated me. I would hear, "You know what? You do not have to deal with all this. Why don't you just check out? It'll be a little bit easier. Just take this way out." I took heed and listened.

I took a handful of some pills on my way to pull the trigger—do I live, or do I die? The enemy kept talking to me and kept talking to me. He was trying to persuade me to pull the trigger. He said, "Just pull the trigger!" So I took the pills. At that moment, after swallowing a handful, I didn't know it then, but I know now that God had a master plan and purpose for my life. I designed and perfected the plan. So much of a plan that I believe He let the Holy Spirit intercept that call. Instantly, an overwhelming fear arose within me, and I just couldn't go through with it. After I took the pills, I immediately went to my mother's room, and I told her that I had a terrible headache, and I took some pills, and I think I took too many. She took me to the hospital, and they received me right away. They began my intake and started taking my vitals. They kept asking me how many pills I took. I said, "I don't know. I just had a headache and was just trying to get rid of it." They gave me a thick liquid to swallow. It was supposed to make me vomit up everything in my system. They watched me and made sure everything was okay. My vitals remained steady, so they sent me home after a few hours.

When I arrived back home, I lay down, and I thought about it. I replayed the crazy, emotionally disturbing day that I had just endured. Then all of a sudden, it was just like the Holy Spirit said, "No, God has something for you. He loves you." The voice said, "God has a plan and a purpose for your life. Don't pull the trigger. Choose to live and not to die. You have to live!"

I was a young girl, a teenager. There was still something in me, something evil-minded, "Russian roulette."

I was inconsolable. I was confused. I chose not to pull the trigger to live and not die. I realized that I did want to live. I had learned as a young child in church that the Word said, "Greater is He that is within me, than He that is in the world." I was trying to learn how to juggle being a happy young teenage girl with all the things that come with going to school. I had hopes of hanging out with friends and liking boys. Being the older sister to four younger siblings, so far, all I looked forward to was attending church weekly.

Now I do have to say that I still had to deal with all that was going on inside, feeling hurt, disappointed, and angry. I was still locked up inside. Yet I was laughing on the outside and living in total hell on the inside. Yesterday kept showing up. I learned to suppress my feelings and my fears from the inside out. Because I still had a choice, I could still pull the trigger. I was conflicted. I didn't want to die. No! I really didn't. "Did you hear me? I don't want to die! I want to live!"

I made a decision that I would never think about pulling the trigger again. I just wanted the pain to go away, and I needed to stop all the chatter in my head. I chose to live.

> But God is faithful, who will not suffer you
> to be tempted above that ye are able but will with
> the temptation also make a way to escape. That
> ye may be able to bear it. (1 Corinthians 10:13)

Chapter 7

Finding Myself in All the Wrong Places

WE LIVED IN some apartments that were in Carson, California. I was about seventeen years old, and one day, I was simply standing outside. I had some shorts on. I inherited my big legs from my mother. There was a guy named Tony. He had two brothers. They were all upstairs, visiting some people that lived in the same apartment building. Apparently, the youngest of the three guys saw me. I found out later, he had said that he liked my big legs. That's what caught his attention.

As he was leaving, he came downstairs, and he spoke to me. He asked me my name and if he could get my phone number. He also asked me if he could call me. I thought he was kind of cute. He had a smooth, velvety dark chocolate complexion. He had a pretty smile and a short curly afro.

I said, "Sure! You can call me." We began to talk. He lived in Inglewood. Inglewood is a city in southwestern Los Angeles County, in California. It is in the Los Angeles metropolitan area, as well as Carson, about twenty minutes away from each other. If you are familiar with Los Angeles, you know the area. We were really from two different worlds. We were opposites that attracted, kind of like the world of darkness and the world of light. I still lived at home with my mom. I was still going to church. I was really involved at that time. I was even singing in the young adult choir. I didn't smoke. I didn't do drugs. I didn't drink or even say curse words. I was trying to do the right thing. He lived at home with his mom and siblings. In their house, his mom was a chain-smoker, and they cursed up a storm. They had potty mouths like sailors. His older siblings, along with his mom, would have plenty of beer or any other alcohol you wanted.

I had gotten a car at that time, so I could visit him. Or if he wanted to come to see me, he was always welcome. I spent more time at their house though because of all the things that were going on in his house, which was nothing like my house. None of those things would ever be allowed. Let me just put it like this, I found myself in a relationship with a guy that smoked weed. I think he was probably about, maybe two or three years older than me. He was out of school, and he had a job. He drank beer, he got high, and he cursed some-times. Those were all things that I despised. Not saying there's any-thing wrong with it if that's what you choose to do—no judgment. Tony did everything that I totally despised. Our spirits were not in agreement. As time went on, being in that type of environment, of course, I got pregnant. I spent more and more time over there. I thought he loved me, and for sure, I loved him. I was beginning to feel different about myself. I guess I thought maybe I was gaining the love from him that I really needed from my father but didn't receive.

As time went on, I found myself in this situation with him, a situation that just didn't sit right with me. It made the house envi-ronment uncomfortable. It was so different than mine. But I stayed because I loved him. I was so uncomfortable. If I went to the store, he wanted me to pick up a pack of cigarettes or a can of beer for him. Trust me, I went out of my way to make sure that the cashier knew it was not for me. Like they really cared. They didn't even know me.

Back in the day, if you got pregnant, your parents insisted that you get married, especially if you attended church. Supposedly, it was the best thing to do. Well, I think it is just a betrayal of the covenant between man and woman to cover up that a sin has been committed. I told them I was not going to marry him. I just felt that he would not have taken care of his responsibilities anyway. Why I felt that way, I don't know. A few girls, some were friends of mine or girls I just went to school with, happened to fall into the same trap and got pregnant. Their parents made them get married at a young age, and unfortunately, it didn't work. They got married for all the wrong reasons. I understood what the adults in my situation were trying to do. What they thought didn't matter to me. I was stubborn enough to say that I was not going to get married and didn't.

We continued our relationship and were blessed with a beautiful baby girl. Two weeks later, I graduated from high school, and I was scheduled to attend college the following fall semester. Fastforward, we experienced some tough times. He acted like he was supportive and understood my quest to learn. I enjoyed learning. I was learning things that I would ultimately turn into my life's passion. I finished too. I graduated with an associate degree in interior design and merchandising.

As time moved forward, Tony and two of his brothers eventually ended up renting a house in Los Angeles, California. I was still me, but I came with a plus one. We were still going together. I would go hang out at their house often. Plus, that was my man, the father of our daughter. Tony had a best friend named Lewis. He was crazy but funny. He was always smiling on my face. Little did I know, the entire time, he was plotting and planning behind my back. One Saturday night, I decided to drop by. I didn't even call him first to let him know. It wasn't strange for me to pop up though. Most of the time, he knew I was coming.

When I walked up to the porch, his oldest brother was at the door. Now that I think about it, I wonder if he was expecting me. He literally opened the door, and he held it open as I walked right in and went straight back. I went straight back to Tony's bedroom, as usual.

Tony was in his bedroom in the middle of getting dressed. He looked like he was about to go out on the town the way he was carefully starching that crease in his pants. There I was, just standing there and watching. I was looking at him crazy because he didn't mention that he was going out. Then again, I didn't call. So I asked, "You're going out?"

He answered me, saying, "Yeah, yeah. I'm just going to go hang out with the fellas."

Interesting, I thought. Of course, I had more questions. After my first level interrogation commenced, he finally told me that Lewis was on his way to come pick him up. If Lewis was picking him up, I knew they would probably hang out all night. Now I wanted to know where they were going. I asked him if he wanted me to stay there until he got back. Was he going to come to my house when they got back later that evening?

Now we were deep into our conversation. I was on round two of my interrogation by the time Lewis arrived. Tony's brother yelled from the living room that Lewis had just pulled up. I was still talking. I assumed Lewis was waiting with his girlfriend in the van because he hadn't come into the house yet. Then Lewis started honking his horn, the rhythmic kind of honk that was hurried but friendly, a sound that indicated that fun was on the horizon. He blew the horn a couple of times, wanting Tony to come outside. I guess he was taking a little bit too long.

I'll never forget it. A young lady appeared out of nowhere and was standing at Tony's door. She was about five feet tall. She was light-complexioned. Her hair was a golden blond color, and she walked right in like she belonged. Suddenly, I got that feeling, that look, that neck rolling, hand on your hip, squinty-eyed, ready to go off kind of look. Her eyes spoke an unspoken ultimatum. As she rolled those eyes, she loudly and boldly said, "Are you coming with us or not?" The silence penetrated the space. It was like watching a scene from a movie. The climactic moment when the main character goes off on someone. We all saw it coming. It unraveled in slow motion. There was a silence, then in unison, the audience said, "Oooooeeeeeee!"

First of all, I've never seen this chick before. So I was trying to figure out not only who she was but also why, at that moment, she was even in the house at all. Where did Tony know her from? Later, I found out that Lewis had introduced her to Tony. She was Lewis's girlfriend's best friend named Rosalyn.

I haven't experienced anything like this before. I was stuck, frozen, and possibly in shock even. It felt as though time was standing still. This journey marker unfolded before my eyes in slow motion. This man/boy turned and looked at me, and then he turned and looked at her. He literally turned toward his bedroom door, walked straight past me, turned down the hallway, and followed that hussy right out the front door. He was like a puppy following a skinny little bone, I mean a skinny bone.

I just was just standing there, dumbfounded and confused. *This isn't happening*, I thought. Who was she? Then it hit me. It was slowly registering in my mind what had just happened. As soon as I realized what was going on, my whole world turned upside down. My heart felt broken. I felt like I couldn't breathe. My heart had been crushed and slammed to the floor. I was devastated. All I could do was stand there, and I cried. His older brother had come into the room by then. He and everyone in the living room had a front-row seat to the event. The look in his eyes when he walked up to me to comfort me, I will never forget. I will also never forget what he said to me. He said, "Tina, I know this hurts, and I know he has broken your heart, but you are a queen, and you deserve better." I thought, *You don't understand. I had this man/boy's baby, and this is what he does, walk right out the door!*

He turned toward me again, and he said, "Tina, I know this is hurting you right now, and you may not understand, but I promise you, you deserve better." What he said next penetrated my spirit. He said, "Him walking out that door is going to be the best thing that ever happened to you." I couldn't stop crying. My sadness was evolving into an ugly cry. I was so emotional. He was very kind with his words. He comforted me some more until I got myself together to drive home. I had to go to work the next day, but I kept calling him because we needed to talk. I needed him to talk to me, explain his side of the story. I would not rest until I found out what was going on with him and her. Needless to say, he never answered my call. I called him consistently for a few more days, and those few days went by. Once I got myself together, I had an epiphany. I thought, *Okay, since you're not answering me, you are answering all my questions.* I made up my mind right then and there. I made the decision that it was over, and I was done. Eventually, about a week later, he called me, but I told him I had nothing to say.

I was impressed with myself. I didn't want my daughter to grow up without her father because, of course, I knew what that felt like. I stood my ground and never went back. As seasons changed and time moved on, he no longer came by to see his daughter. He didn't come by at all. His family eventually stopped coming over to see her too. It became a one-sided situation. They wanted me to just continue to bring her over to see them for a visit. I made an attempt. I made it clear that they were welcome to come and get her any time they wanted. I felt since we were not together anymore, there was no need for me to entertain the back and forth. As far as I was concerned, I was done.

Some time has passed now. I have gotten married and moved to Palmdale, California. One day, I had gone to Gardena, a city adjacent to Los Angeles, to visit my in-laws. It was a little over an hour's drive from where I lived. I knew though that while I was in the area, I would visit one of my favorite stomping grounds. I was headed to the Roadium Open-Air Market. The locals called it "The Rodeo." The novelty of this place is that it is on the property of a classic, throwback, drive-in theatre. It is a fifteen-acre open-air market that offers a miscellaneous mix of new and used underground urban furniture, clothing, and jewelry. Treasures and ideas can be found down several aisles and beyond. You would always check there first for whatever you may be looking for. For generations, it has always been the go-to spot.

My daughter was about six years old, and we were walking down the rug aisle. I was looking for a simple runner for the walkway, and I heard somebody call my name. "Tina! Tina!" Of course, I thought, *Who is this calling me? Who knows that I'm here? I don't even live out here anymore?* I was more than surprised when I turned around, and it was Tony, standing at the gold jewelry counter, with her. He was still with Rosalyn. He came right over to where my daughter and I were standing. While he was saying hello to us, I looked at my baby, looking up into his eyes. I realized that when she spoke back to him, she was saying hi to a stranger.

Notice, I said, "My daughter." He was a stranger to her. She didn't even know who he was. He said, "I tried to get in contact with you, but I heard you got married."

I told him, "Yes, but the number hasn't changed. I have the same phone number, and I have no missed calls from you. I had lived in the same house with my mother up until the day I got married, July 24! Therefore, I am not listening to any excuses from you about trying to get in contact with me!" Clearly, there were more than a few words that needed to be exchanged.

Then, as if he could, he asked the million-dollar question, "Why did you marry him anyway?" He was speaking about my husband, Clifton.

Him? I thought. *He didn't even know "him!"* I was more than happy to accommodate Tony with an answer to that very question. "Because he loved me the way I loved you. That's why I married him!"

Tony was silent. He couldn't say anything because he knew how much I loved him. It was at that point that Miss Thang walked up to where we were standing. It was obvious that she still felt the need to let me know that she was still with him. I decided not to waste any more of my time. I looked at her, and I looked at him. I turned around, and I walked away. My daughter said, "Mommy, who was that man?"

I said, "Oh, that was just somebody that I knew from back in the day. Let's go look at these mirrors."

I felt like a million-dollar. It was at that moment I knew him walking out that door then was the best thing that ever happened to me. I was proud of myself. I walked away from our past with no regrets. I walked away with a newfound respect for my journey. I began looking forward to my tomorrow. Baby girl and I were just fine.

I called it finding myself in all the wrong places because sometimes, as young girls or women, we tend to settle for less. Before I woke up and realized who I was, I had to be reminded of who I was.

I had to be reminded that I am the daughter of the Most High King. I don't have to settle for less ever again. Like I said earlier, I was dating a guy that drank. He smoked cigarettes and weed. The way he used profanity was like a secondary secret language. The way he would put words together was a little pimpish. But those words, those calculated words, they could make a weaker person respond differently.

We were not equally yoked, so little did I know back then, he was never really an option anyway. Now I know that. I grew up in a Christian home. He lived a lifestyle that I really didn't need to be a part of. I guess I was seeking love. I was trying to fill the void of my father not stepping up to the plate and being a responsible and dependable father. Every little girl's fantasy dad is a superhero.

After that relationship, I knew what I wanted and what I didn't want. I learned to make a list. I made a list of some of the characteristics and qualities and morals that I wanted out of a man and what type of relationship that I wanted to be in from that point forward.

Chapter 8

Now I Lay Me Down to Sleep

NOW I LAY me down to sleep. I pray the Lord my soul will keep. If I die before I wake, I pray the Lord my soul he will take. When I think about this simple child's prayer, "Now I lay me down to sleep," it takes my mind back to a time in my life that was very dark, a time in my life that kind of wrapped me up and entangled me in bondage. I found myself in a place lying down to sleep, a place that I never thought that I would be. I was in love with a man that was actually, I believe, not in love, but in lust with me.

In my relationship with Tony, there were so many disappointing moments. Not only did I have one abortion, but also I had two abortions. I felt so conflicted because this unexpected necessity on my journey totally went against everything I believe in. I grew up in the church, so fornication and abortion went against everything that I was taught.

I found myself entangled in something that I despise. It ate me alive. I walked around, holding so much inside. The times I felt strong, I wanted to say something. But then I would hear Satan, the enemy, tell me, "You can't even talk about that. You are a Christian woman. How is that going to make you look?" The thought that I had an abortion not once but twice destroyed me inside.

I already had a little one. Back then, I knew Tony wasn't ready for the other two. I had to live with that nightmare, the thought of how I walked around with an embryo living inside of me, growing and becoming, being nourished by my body. I held in such a deep dark secret. Not only was I fornicating, but I was also responsible for their murder, not once but twice. My body was supposed to be used as a temple. My body was supposed to be a holy sacrifice unto God.

Time had gone on, and now I am married to Clifton. I would cover up my pain through silence, triggered by the memory of my sin. In some of those times, he would ask me, "Are you okay?" Every time I wanted to speak to my husband, I felt like a little girl in the classroom that wanted to speak up but was too shy. I raised my hand in my mind, but then the enemy would be right there. He would say, "No, no, no, baby girl, you can't talk about that! You are a Christian woman! How are you going to tell your business and admit to the sins you have committed?" That inside voice haunted me for years. I walked around like everything was okay though. On the outside, I was smiling. But when I was triggered by something I saw on TV or if I saw a certain commercial, I would be silent. I had not taken the time to deal with that trauma. I would just respond and say that I was okay, but on the inside, it tore me up. I didn't know if I would be able to have a baby again or not because I don't know what those people did to my body at the clinic. It was such a heavy burden to carry that fear alone. I didn't know if it was really a legit place. I guess it was legit. I didn't really know what they were doing to my body. I remember the feeling, the feeling of someone vacuuming out my insides, my embryos, my babies. They were sucking a life out of me, a baby, my baby that I had to give up because of Tony.

I say now I lay me down to sleep because I lay on that table, and it was a nightmare, and I didn't think that I was ever going to wake up. It wasn't until I put my hand in God's hand, and I cried out to him and allowed Him to step in. I cried out to Him, and I said, "God, I need some help! I am in bondage! I feel shackled, and I want to be free." And that's when He stepped in, and He began to remove the layers of all that I was carrying.

I prayed until I found myself at a place where I just woke up. I came to my senses, and I asked God for forgiveness. I repented before His throne. I came to myself, and I took those shackles off. I knew I was free when I began to speak freely. I began to walk in the liberty that God had set before me. No longer was I "laying me down to sleep." From that nightmare, I woke up. I began to share my testimony with other young girls and women. I would speak to them about having an abortion. I have supported women at the cusps of their life-changing moment. I literally got to a place that I would get on my knees, begging some girls not to have an abortion. I would plead with them while explaining the hell, the torment, and the nightmares that I had to live with. I just didn't want anybody else to go through what I had endured, so I found my voice, and I spoke out.

The Word does tell us that the "enemy comes to steal, kill, and destroy." He doesn't care how he does it, just as long as he does it. Walking around with the hell of being tormented and the trauma from the nightmares can literally destroy you mentally. I was so adamant that, thank God, most of them decided not to lay their babies down to sleep. They woke up to a new reality. They decided to either keep their babies or give them up in an open adoption.

Chapter 9

Family Matters

FAMILY TO ME is so important. They are my foundation, the core of who I am. I am the oldest of five. I have one sister and three brothers. The relationship that I have with my siblings is like most. We have a special kind of unspoken bond. We don't always get along, but we have each other's back, even if we have a disagreement among ourselves. If something were to go down with one of us, if a thang, thang was to go down in them streets, whether we needed backup or not, we have always had each other's back. We have laughed together with or about each other, which is what we do best. We have cried together, and we have prayed for each other. Back in the day, we would fight verbally and physically. As the oldest, some may know this from experience, not just hearsay, especially those that proudly hold that title too. You know, there are a lot of responsibilities piled on to your back.

My mom and dad divorced when I was very young. When my mom remarried, my siblings were born. That marriage dissolved, so mom became a single mother, raising five children. She is a strong woman, so she did just what she had to do in order to provide for her family. It's always hard when the fathers are around, and then suddenly, they abandon you, with children to raise, three young men at that. Needless to say, I, too, had kids to raise. I was the oldest.

Let me paint the picture for you. During this time, our ages were twelve, nine, eight, one, and one. So there was a wide-ranging age difference. I was the oldest.

My sister Delandria is three years younger than me. My brother Darren is four years younger. When I was twelve, my mom, having remarried, was blessed with a set of twin boys, Shawn and Shannon. Mother continued to work. She had to provide for her family. I was the surrogate, the go-to. We were a team, but the littles kept me busy.

My mom was the best. We had a beautiful home that stayed clean. She had a knack for decorating. I always loved the way she would mix certain colors. Our house was always exquisitely decorated. One of my jobs was to make sure it stayed that way. Our friends and neighbors would always be surprised when they came over. I am not sure what they expected. There were a lot of us, but that is "no excuse for a nasty house," Momma would always say. Once they saw how she decorated it, we would always end up giving a tour. They were so visually stimulated. They wanted to see more. She loved color and was not afraid of it. So we were very proud and had no problem inviting people over.

For the holidays, she would lavish us with so much. She would almost, over gift if that's possible. Her giving heart manifested through her hard work. Her efforts were never in vain. We loved it. We have always shown her our appreciation in return. She was always giving to other kids in the neighborhood, too, especially if they had even a little less than we did. I know her giving spirit taught me to be a giver. That's why to this day, I love giving from my heart too.

My mom is a very Christian woman, and as you know, we grew up in the church. One thing that has always been true, God is always first. My relationship with my heavenly Father is even closer now because of that. For this, I am grateful. My mother is amazing. She is an organized person, and she is very creative. I am more than sure that the gene has been passed down to me. I will be the spokesperson for our crew, too, when I say, "She is a remarkable woman!" We wanted for nothing. She made sure of that.

As I was preparing my notes for this memorialization of my good and bad, one of my brothers suggested that I include their words and sentiments. I agree. So I decided to look forward to sharing the thoughts of my family, discussing how they saw me from their perspective. I think that sharing their thoughts would allow a bird's eye view of who I was and who I am today. "Will the real McCoy please stand up? Tina Andrea, come stand front and center to hear what they had to say about you, girl! Now, listen, Linda, listen!"

Mother

Being your mother is a gift. You, my daughter, are a marvelous gift. As a little girl, you were always busy. You would be so curious about anything and everything you put your hands on. I should have known then that you were going to make a mark on this world. For your sister and brothers, there was nothing you wouldn't do to make sure they were safe and okay.

You have always set a good example for them, showing them a positive path to follow in life. You are an amazing daughter, mother, grandmother, and friend to everyone that has become a part of your life. The most important thing, my beautiful daughter, is you are a fighter and survivor. When the storms of life kept ragging in your life, you spoke to the hurricanes, earthquakes, and the pain and proclaimed, "Peace be still! It's already done!"

As a true woman of God, I am excited for you, and I want you to know that I am patiently waiting to see manifested the great things God has in store. I look forward to the next chapter in your life. So I say to you, daughter, you keep redefining beauty every time you smile. Let your light so shine. You command respect by knowing your worth. You are phenomenal in every aspect of your life. I color you, daughter, with my love.

Mother

My Baby Sister

My sister is the most giving person I know. She definitely has my back, no matter what, which is funny because I thought she couldn't stand me when we were younger. I realized to her back in those days, she was like my second momma. Being a single parent of five, my mom had to work a lot. Tina, basically, had to step up and stand in for her while she was working. To be honest, I would not have liked me either. As we have gotten older, we have developed a very strong sister bond, and I would not give that up for the world. I can always tell how good a person is by who shows up in a time of need. The outpour of love, kind sentiments, and gestures she received while she walked through her medical challenge said it all. Besides that, anybody that would give all their birthday gifts to a women's domestic violence shelter has to be a gift themselves.

Love, Delandria, aka Dee

My Younger Brother

When I was younger, Tina was my big sister, but to me, she was more like a mother figure. Momma worked a lot. She was a single parent, raising five kids. Back in those days, it was even more difficult. I know that Momma always did the best she could to provide for us. Tina had to step up and help out because she was the oldest. She was the one my mother had to lean on to help keep us and our home together. She was the most mature. I don't remember her smiling at all when I was a child. I recall that she seemed to look mean, especially in day-to-day situations.

I can barely remember her being happy. I don't recall seeing her smile that much, only on occasion, like holidays. I believe Delandria and I used to call her "Mean Tina" as we were growing up. I don't know how much of that changed. We had a somewhat tight sister and brother relationship, mainly because she was focused on what she had to do. She had so many responsibilities. As we got older, I saw how willing and focused she would always be when it came to helping others. She tries to teach people how to be better people.

She is a very spiritual woman. She is very giving and gives from the heart, it seems, with no expectation of return. She is very kind. If she says she is going to do something, whatever it is, she is going to do it. If she wants your help or needs your help, she will ask you, but she won't beg you. If you can do it, fine. If you can't, fine. For sure, it is still going to get done.

She is the type of person that you could go to if you need to borrow some money. She would lend you the money, not expecting to get it back.

She grew up to be a beautiful woman, always helping other people. She raised her kids then helped out her siblings with their children. She and my mother have lived together for years. Who does that? I mean, a lot of people do it, but there are a lot of people who can't do it because it is not for everybody—the things I have seen Tina go through, and she is still standing. Like the Bible says, "When you have done all you could, just stand."

Her belief and faith in God are so pure and tight. You know that you have gone through one thing just to get to another. Whatever it is, you know that He's got you, and you believe it.

Sometimes, I know that is hard to do. But no matter what, you had always had the same face, even when you were in the midst of the storm. You never changed. You are one of the strongest nicest people I have ever seen. You are the best person I know. I have never seen you do bad. I have never seen you wish ill will or hurt toward anyone. No matter what, you always did things the right way.

Love, Darren

My Baby Brother

I remember you being like a second mother. Actually, I think Shannon and I called you Mom at one time. What I do know is, we feared you like you were our mom. Because of Mom's work schedule, you took care of all of us. You were stern but not abusive. I don't remember you hitting us, looking back now. You were very mature for your age too. We were supposed to just be kids. I remember one time, back in the day, I played baseball for the Dolphin Park youth team. I was so excited to play ball that day, so I was trying to leave the house at eight o'clock that morning. My game was around one o'clock, maybe noon at the earliest. Tina stopped me because my uniform was still filthy from the last game. Here I was, walking out the front door. She stopped me and told me to go wash it first, but I didn't. I actually snuck out of the house, headed to Dolphin Park. Do you know that Tina ended up walking to the park and snatched my behind right up? She marched me back home and made me wash my uniform like she told me in the first place. It was at that moment, I knew she really loved us. But she did not play games.

That was forty years ago though. Today, she has become the power force that we all knew she would become, one of the strongest people I know, spiritually and mentally. She is a go-getter. Her work ethic is unlike anything I've ever seen. I've asked for favors, and she has never told me no. Tina is the glue that holds us together. To this day, we have a great relationship, and the love between us is stronger than ever. Thanks, big sis!

Love, Shawn

My Other Younger Brother

I had to laugh out loud when Shawn told me that story. That is exactly how I remembered it too. Tina used to roll her tongue back and smack her lips while whooping our butts. All it took was for us to not listen to what she said or to not do what she told us to do. If we got out of line, I do remember getting hit. That really makes me laugh out loud. I just know we would not have survived without her nurturing, guidance, and love. She is our matriarch. She is definitely my inspiration.

Love, Shanon

I love my brothers and sister deeply. Even though we are all older now, we still make sure we are there for each other and for each other's children and grandchildren. Sometimes in life, unexpected things happen. When one of us is in need, we make sure that we try to fulfill that need. We are all we have. We will continue to stick together. We are family, and family matters.

Chapter 10

My Happily Ever Not So After

The Beginning

THIS IS WHERE my "happily ever" began. It was Saturday night, March 6, 1981. I was twenty-one years old. I had gone to a club in Los Angeles called Carolina West. Even then, it was considered a club from "back in the day." LA had a lot of spots like that. One of my godsisters and our mutual friend had come into town. Tony and I had just broken up, so I was not hanging out or seeing anyone around that time. I was focused on working and taking care of my baby. I didn't even feel like being bothered, especially to go out. They were so excited to go clubbing in LA. They talked me into it. I really didn't care where we went because I didn't want to go. Since I decided to be nice and spend time with my family, I had one stipulation. I was driving my own car so that when I was ready to leave, I could go. I know how it goes—the later it gets, everybody starts hooking up. Nope, I was not staying out late at all.

Here we were at the Carolina West. It was packed. It was an urban club of mixed ages. Tonight was lady's night, so the wolves were in the building. Ladies got in free before a certain time in those days. While we were in line, I kept looking at my watch, hoping we would make it through the line in time. I had ten dollars, and I was trying not to spend it. Plus, we were probably going to get food too. My crew and I were in the line, laughing and having fun. There was a guy that had on one of those sweaters that the guys were wearing in the '80s. He just kept smiling at my friend. He was kind of cute, but it was dark, and we were already near the front. She had on this acid-washed outfit that she got from the swap meet the last time she came to visit. Her jean jacket had those long fringes. I had just pressed and curled her hair before we left, so she was feeling it.

We made it inside, and it was packed. There was a spot in the club near the back where people could play pool. A lot of the cute guys seemed to hang out in this area because it was near the bar, right across from the dance floor. I thought about being glad I came. Everyone looked good, smelled good, and rocked to the music in unison, except by the end of the night, I would end up with a stalker. For the majority of the night, there was a guy that decided I was his future, so he followed me around everywhere.

I was attempting to dodge this guy the entire night. He didn't even care that I could see how obvious he was. Truthfully, I wasn't sure how he thought he even had a chance. He was nerdy acting, but he thought he was cool—the guy dancing around in the mirror by himself, that guy. He had been stalking me the whole night.

As soon as I decided I was glad I came, they started playing slow songs. So I took the opportunity to visit the ladies' room. I put some more gloss on and fixed my baby hair. There were two girls in there, talking a bit loud, and it seemed like they were getting louder. I quickly washed my hands. I didn't take my time either, just in case. Wouldn't you know it, as soon as I came out, there he was. He was trying to look inconspicuous standing by the pay phone that was next to the men's bathroom. I started to yell, "I see you, duh!" But my momma raised me right, and lucky for him, someone got his attention. I took that moment to politely walk to the left, right out the door and headed straight toward the pool tables. I had left the girls near the dance floor.

I stood, watching the guys playing pool for a minute. From where I was standing, I could see my godsister on the dance floor, slow dancing with the cute guy that we saw when we were in the

line earlier. Clifton was one of the guys playing pool. He was with a
few of his friends too. They were really into the game when I walked
up. They were laughing hard and being loud. As I scanned the area,
I noticed that I kept catching his eye. When I would look at him,
he was already looking at me. He didn't even try to play it off. He
seemed to not care. He just kept staring at me. I started feeling a little
nervous. I used to be quiet and a little shy when I was younger. At the
same time, I wasn't surprised that he couldn't take his eyes off of me.
I had on a cream V-neck sweater, and I wore a collared shirt under it.
It was colorful, too, because I had it perfectly coordinated with my
light peach corduroy gaucho pants. I did look cute.

I stood there, feeling a little shaky because I was thinking,
Seriously, why is this man watching me? I did a mental check and
adjusted my clothes and patted my hair a little bit, just in case I
had morphed into a monster since the last time I went to the ladies'
room. I thought maybe my pants were unzipped or something. I
didn't know what was going on, but I was beginning to feel awkward.
During this time, my stalker had made his way over to the pool tables
and was heading in my direction. The stalker noticed that something
had me distracted. I could tell from his expression. He, too, was trying to figure out what Clifton was looking at. I saw him see me see
him, and I did a quick 180 turn and headed toward my friends. I
could still see them from where I was. By then, they were waving me
over from where they were sitting, on the other side of the club, near
the VIP section. I left Clifton there, pretending to play pool because
apparently, he was still watching me. I would later hear from his
friends that they were getting mad and teasing him that night. He
had stopped playing pool, and I guess he kept watching me, so they
were giving him a hard time. Clifton said he put the pool stick down,
took the $25 in quarters he had just won, and headed toward the VIP
section. He was seeking to find me. He had just won a lot of money.
It was time to celebrate. The way Clifton was looking at me on-site,
it was clear that cupid's arrow had landed.

To be honest, I never believed that there was such a thing as a
"cupid's arrow" moment. But I saw it firsthand myself, that night it
happened to Clifton. Come to find out, Clifton and my godsister

had attended the same high school, so they knew each other. He went to her to get the 411 about me. She gave him all the tea. He knew that I was single and that I had broken up with my boyfriend Tony recently. She gave him an earful about me. Of course, she took great pleasure in coming to tell me things about him. She made sure that I knew he had a good job and that he made good money, with no children. The bottom line though, he wanted to talk to me.

As I thought about what she was telling me, I decided, because I was ready to go, that Clifton could walk me to my car. I had to work the next day, and, of course, the girls wanted to stay a little bit longer. My car was parked about a block away, and it was getting late, so, I said, "Clifton, would you walk me to my car, please?" He hopped at the invitation. As we walked toward my car, we talked some more. During our conversation, he asked me where I worked since I told him I had to go in the next day, and I proceeded to ask him about his job. Once we finally arrived at my car, he was a gentleman. He opened my door, and we exchanged phone numbers. I noticed he didn't write my number down though. He simply said, "I'll call you sometime," and walked away. I got in my car, and I took the twenty-minute drive from Los Angeles to the city of Carson, where I lived. I was thinking to myself on my drive how most of the men that were in that club were all probably collecting phone numbers from as many women as they could. By the time Clifton got to my phone number, I am sure I would not remember who he was. I didn't think anything else about Clifton that night.

It was Sunday morning, and I made it to work on time but sleepy. I worked at R&B Furniture, a store in Gardena. I went to college for interior design, so I loved working there. A couple of hours had passed into my shift. I was walking around the store being busy, fluffing the pillows and making adjustments to a few displays. I looked up from where I was standing while dusting a table, and in walked Clifton. My mouth dropped. Thank goodness, no one was in the store at that moment because I was startled, surprised, and excited, so I shouted, "What are you doing here!"

Clifton responded, "Well, I didn't believe that you worked here, so I stopped by to see if you did."

I was shocked. All I could say was "Oh my goodness, oh my goodness!"

He said, "What time is your lunch break?"

My breaks weren't that long, and I knew there was a McDonald's right up the street. So I proceeded to get my purse from the back. I put on some gloss and checked my baby hair. Most of the food places were far away, so I suggested that we go down the street to McDonald's because my lunch break was not that long. We got our food, and we sat down and talked. He was asking me about me, then I returned his questions with the same questions. I thought he was kind of cute because he had the biggest smile. He spoke in a calm, cool tone that made me comfortable. He was one year older than me. He was about to turn twenty-two in the next two days. I said, "Wow, happy birthday!" We talked about me a little more because he made it clear he wanted some details. Our conversation evolved, and we started talking about our proms for some reason. That ended up being the door that was opened for me to let him know that I had a daughter that was almost three years old. I told him how I was pregnant at my prom. He simply looked at me with a straight face for a half second, then we just continued our conversation. Once that was out of the way, I felt a little relieved because I wanted to make everything clear by letting him know that there were two of us. He just said, "Okay, I'm gonna call you."

For all the following week, he attempted to reach me. He kept calling, and I kept missing him because I was getting off of work late. I got off at nine in the evening, and I didn't get home until about 9:45 p.m. When I would get home, my sister would always meet me at the door, saying, "That boy Clifton keeps calling here for you." I started to feel bad, but I had already told him that I didn't get home until about 9:45 p.m. For some reason, Clifton still thought I was giving him the runaround, so he was being very persistent. We were eventually able to connect, and we began to talk. He told me he was trying to do things differently with me. Normally, he would not date a young lady that had children because he didn't want the baby mama/baby daddy drama. That wasn't my situation, so he said he wanted to meet up. He said he would give it a try because he was drawn to me, and he was willing to see what happens.

Another week had passed. Time kept on ticking when you are a young working mother. Finally, this time, when we spoke, I decided to invite him over. It would be our second time meeting in person. He showed up on my off day though. I believe it was a Friday, and I was in the middle of coloring my hair. Well, I've been doing it myself since I was about at least fifteen years old. While growing up, it was normal to have kitchen beauticians in the family. I did not spend my money at the hair salon. A honey-golden blond was my color choice back in the day. When he came in, I said, "Well, you're here. You might as well help me color my hair," not knowing at the time that he had four sisters.

Things began to feel more comfortable. We were officially talking. Clifton began coming over to my house every day. I met him on March 6. I remember because it was two days before his birthday. Now we were in the middle of June. I was at work one day, and Clifton showed up, saying he wanted to take me to lunch. On my break, we went down to a park that was close to the job. He had already stopped by Kentucky Fried Chicken and bought lunch before he picked me up. They had the best biscuits. When we got out of the car, we held hands and walked over to a grassy area. He laid down a blanket that he had brought with him. I sat down as he laid out our lunch. While he was down on one knee, he proceeded to propose. He pulled out a ring box and everything. I have to say it was so romantic. I must give him his props. He was just so smooth with it too. Of course, I was shocked! I said, "Oh my goodness, yes!" I accepted the proposal. What! Am I getting married?

I found out a while later that he had already spoken with my mom and asked her if he could marry me. No wonder he kept coming over. She gave him her permission. Now engaged, he and I were spending so many hours together. Everything just connected and worked out. He would go to work, finish work, leave early, and then come back to my house every night. We talked about our dreams. We talked about our desires and goals, the things we wanted out of life. After he proposed, we decided to get married the following year, July 24, 1982.

"Yes, I do!"

This is how it, we, came together. We met in March, he proposed in June, and then we got married in July of the following year. This is why I said this man fell in love with me at first sight. He wasted no time, and it was all okay with me because I fell for him too. The following year, we had a huge wedding. After the wedding, we had fun, and it felt like we were the perfect couple. We were so in love and happy. The plan was to move into a house that Clifton's sister was selling. That deal fell through though. Subsequently, we lost all the money that we had saved because we had put the money we had in the house. The house was sold, but we didn't benefit.

Once we got married, his parents felt bad about how we lost out on our home, especially because we had nowhere to go. All this unfolded days before the wedding. They allowed us to move in with them so we could start saving our money all over again. We saved money, and we stayed, knowing that we had a plan. We were going to buy a home.

One of Clifton's older sisters, Geneva, worked in aerospace. She was a supervisor at that time for Rockwell International. She said they were hiring, and she could get me on full time with benefits. She had just moved out to the city of Lancaster in the Antelope Valley. At that time, I worked for Pacific Bell, the telephone company. We decided to take on the challenge of relocating, and we gratefully accepted the opportunity. We knew it was going to put us in a better position as a new family. I moved in with Clifton's sister, Geneva, and her family for a few months. She was married with three children, and I became her daughter's buddy. She was ten. Believe it or not, we enjoyed each other's company. She was always so happy to see me. Kelly and I are very close to this day. We lived in Lancaster, which was twenty minutes from Palmdale. Clifton and our daughter stayed at his parents' house in Compton, which is further South, right outside of Los Angeles. During the week, our daughter went to McKinley Elementary, which was across the street, near the corner of where they lived. Clifton went to that school, and my baby had his former teacher. This was so convenient in a lot of ways. She was in kindergarten, so I felt good knowing my baby was safe and well taken care of.

I took the job at Rockwell International, which was in the city of Palmdale, about 70 miles north of Los Angeles. I would travel back and forth to Compton on Friday nights after work or Saturday mornings. Then I would return to Lancaster on Sunday nights. I don't remember how long I commuted. I did that for a while though, and every Sunday, when I had to leave my family because I had to go to work, I would cry all the way home. I didn't want to leave my husband and my daughter, but I knew that it was for the best because we were going to be gaining a home. Clifton had already been working for the county of Los Angles, so he had a full-time job with benefits too. We were cutting corners and being conservative with our spending, saving as much as we could to buy our home, especially during that time because homes in the Antelope Valley were very inexpensive in the '80s. After saving for almost two years, in May of 1984, we purchased our first home. It was a single-story home, but it was covered in red brick, and we loved it. I wanted my house to be picture perfect. I was so excited because I had gone to college for interior design, and Clifton let me decorate it just the way that I wanted. I went all out. I had so many creative ideas. It could have easily been in a magazine.

Eventually, Clifton transferred jobs from Los Angeles to work in the Antelope Valley. He was still with Los Angeles county, but now he worked for the waterworks department. We were very happy with this decision because he used to commute to Long Beach, about 90 miles away, and he worked the second shift. I was not comfortable with the hours he had to travel to get home at night. We had a second child, our son, and life was good. We had the brick house, we had two nice cars, we were a two-income household, and we had benefits. We even had life insurance. We were adulting, and we were on our way. We were "happily ever after." We still drove "down below" to Los Angeles on Sundays to attend church. I had joined Clifton's family church near his mother's home in Compton. It was the church that his family attended his entire life. My husband was the baby boy of the family. Now for a sidebar—Clifton had been born into the Pentecostal church but had never accepted the plan of salvation nor the Lord as his personal Savior. I found out from his sister when he was thirty years old, seven years into our marriage, that Clifton was never saved.

Now back to the story. Clifton began to work on the weekend, and he was too tired to drive down on Sundays. I had a coworker that invited me to a church that was in Littlerock, about thirty minutes away. I did not want to drive down below with the kids by myself, so I accepted the invitation and visited her church. I found myself visiting often, so I eventually became a member. Clifton continued to work on Saturday, then he would often be too tired on Sunday to go to church. I could see that there was a change. After about five years, I desired to have a bigger home. Now mind you, I am the type of person that if I am on a mission to accomplish something, it usually happens. I had faith in this mission. I didn't yet know the how or when, but I truly believed because I could see it manifesting. I could imagine all the little details coming together, and they did. Through this urge for a bigger home, Clifton learned quickly that I would not give up until it came to pass. I guess we had that in common, thinking about how he pursued me relentlessly.

As time went on, I began to actively start looking for a house. I told Clifton that "the house" was in our same neighborhood, a couple of blocks over. I was excited about this one because we wanted the children to still attend the same school. Interestingly, we purchased our first home when we were twenty-four and twenty-five. Now we have settled in our second home. Clifton has begun to hang out with some of the people from work, and now he started going to the gym. He was invited to events that some of the people had, but he would never invite me to go with him. I was never his plus one. He would say, "Oh, there will be a lot of drinking and smoking there, and I know you won't like to be around that." This was true, so I had no problem with him going without me. I began to see a little change in Clifton after he started hanging out with those people and going to that gym. He didn't have time for church at all anymore, even though the kids and I continued to go every Sunday. By this time, I was very active in the church too.

As the years passed, we began to allow ourselves to travel. We would go to a couple of places here and there. I was content, no complaints, life was just good, I thought. My mom had to come live with us out of necessity for a few minutes, so I knew then, we would need to get a bigger home. I was thinking of a two-story home this time. We had already lived in our second home for about eight and a half years by then, so it was time. I told Clifton. I simply said, "We're going to move, and we're going to need to get a bigger house." He knew once I put my mind to it, once I spoke it, then that is exactly what would happen, and it did. Operation third house it was, and I took off running in my search. Needless to say, I found a two-story home in Palmdale that was brand-new. This home would be the first home to be purchased after having been built from the ground up. We were elated and excited. We thought we were living the dream.

Clifton continued to go to that gym, and he soon became a personal trainer there. As a result, he was gone from home more than ever. He always made time for us to travel though. We began traveling, going on vacation with his sister Renee and her husband, Enrique. She was the youngest in his family. I have known her as my sister for most of my life, and they became our travel buddies. We were like four peas in a pod. We enjoyed each other's company, and we were entertained by the same things. We traveled to exotic locations and participated in excursions and different activities while on vacation, except Clifton and I did not do the snorkeling with them. I tried it once, and I felt like I was going to have a nervous breakdown in the water. I do have to say, I was able to have a guide teach me on one trip to Mexico. It helped that they snorkeled with me, and I did pretty good. I didn't even panic. I was so proud of myself and my in-loves, our besties, were too.

I mean, God created this world, and I wanted to see every inch of it. We went from A to Z around the globe—from Antigua, Arizona, Aruba, Bahamas, Barbados, Belize, Cabo San Lucas, Cancún, Curacao, Colorado, Costa Rica, Cozumel, Dominica, Dominican Republic, Ensenada, Fiji, Florida, Georgia, Grand Canyon, Grand

Cayman, Grand Turk's, Haiti, Honduras, Ise de Rotan, Italy, Jamaica, Kauai, Kenya, Kona, Los Cabos, Maryland, Mazatlán, Oahu, Paris, Puerto Rico, Puerto Vallarta, Rome, Spain, St. John, St. Kitt, St. Lucía, St Martin, St. Thomas, Tahiti, Texas, Virginia, and Washington, DC. We have gone on eleven cruises around the world. We all really enjoyed doing that. Together, we have experienced the top of the Eiffel Tower in Paris, and we've walked on the bottom of the ocean in Cabo San Lucas. I have ridden a camel in Los Cabos, and I have zip-lined in the rain forest of the Dominican Republic. I have even luxuriated on a raft down a lazy river in Jamaica. We have gone on a leisure stroll near the ocean, on the backs of horses, across sandy beaches. I have felt black sand between my toes. I have seen white and even all pink sandy beaches, as I've walked and frolicked on international islands. We visited the Palace of Versailles. We para-sailed over the ocean in Mazatlán. I have toured the inside of the Colosseum in Rome and walked inside the Leaning Tower of Pisa. I am blessed to say the adventures went on and on.

Our motto was "You only live once, but if you do this thing called life right, once is enough." We were fulfilling the dreams that we had, and all our desires were manifesting. We did not dream about the life we wanted to live. We lived the life of our dreams. We usually took two-three vacations a year, and we would travel the world. Once we came home though, we went our separate ways. In addition to his work at that gym, Clifton also drove big trucks for a friend of his named Anthony. Anthony purchased mobile homes out of state to flip. He would bring them back to California, renovate them, then sell them. Clifton had the necessary licensing to haul big loads, so he would go out of town with him to help him drive the trucks. Quick sidenote, Clifton would also go to Las Vegas from time to time with "the guys" from his old job. Clifton went back to his long hours at the gym, leaving very little quality time for just him and me. When I would want to just hang out with friends or doing something locally, just he and I, he would always comment on how I wasn't satisfied that we had just taken a beautiful vacation. From the outside looking in, our "happy wife, happy life" facade was intact, but I was not at all happy with how things were between us.

One evening in particular, while standing in my kitchen, I looked toward the family room, and a big snake was slithering across the floor, headed toward the kitchen, near where I was standing, so random and unexpected, of course. I do live in the High Desert though, and I did have the backdoor open while I did some backyard purging over the last few days. I panicked, and I was frozen. I was able to scream out to my son to come to me. Urgently, of course, he came racing down the stairs. I am sure my shrill had his adrenaline pumping as he came down on a mission to save his momma from whatever danger was looming. Once he accessed the situation, he rushed off to get the shovel. He intended to kill the snake. When he returned, after what felt like a million minutes, he had the shovel in hand. I love my son. He was being so brave. This was one of many moments to come where he would play this role. He was the man of the house in his father's absence. Upon approach, with a substantially accurate chop down, he successfully decapitated the snake. The snake's body was ready to fight though. It flopped and squirmed while I screamed and jumped around. I was completely grossed out. Visually, it really felt upsetting to my spirit. It felt like the enemy itself had penetrated my perfect fortress through its seemingly dark visitation. I said, "Oh my goodness, the enemy has crawled into my house!" I immediately began to pray, and I started pleading the blood of Jesus over my home.

I will never forget this. It was in October 2010. I was going over our phone bill. We were on a family plan, and recently, I noticed my daughter had been making a lot of calls way more than usual because it affected our usage and data allowance. So in my probe to dissect the phone bill and the source of these calls, there was one number that stood out. It was repeated on several pages of the bill at different times during the day. There was no actual pattern, so I paid attention. Clifton was in his man cave upstairs for the evening, his favorite spot when he was home. I went upstairs, and I approached him with the phone bill in hand. I asked him if he knew who the numbers belonged to. I was going to show him the numbers that seemed excessive. But it was clear that he was not happy. He didn't like me questioning at all, ever, about anything. So I prepared myself to have this round. You know that thing called intuition? Well, my "spidey senses" were tingling, and I was seeing red flags in his tone and mannerism. He sat up in his chair and looked me square in the eye and said, "That is one of my client's numbers!"

All I could say was "Okay," especially since I never showed him the number(s). He was seemingly frustrated and wanted to see the numbers. I had to think quick because now it began the foolery, the "you must think I'm stupid!" thoughts.

Refusing to give him the bill, I ran into the bedroom, slamming the door behind me as he yelled through the door. I quickly wrote down the phone number then snatched opened the door and gave him the bill. I proceeded to my home office downstairs, straight to the computer. I took the number that I had written down, and like an investigator, I entered the numbers in anticipation of what would soon pop up on the screen. The number was assigned to a female named Tammy Willis. My first thought was "Okay, he said it was his client, and he does have female clients." He was a personal trainer. Just in case, I wrote down Tammy's address and cell phone number. I did my due diligence in searching for anything I could find because something just didn't sit right in my spirit. I wasn't really sure what it was, so just in case, I took the piece of paper with the information that I had written down. I went upstairs to my closet. I put the paper in an old wallet that I had not gotten around to throwing away, and I said, "God, whatever this is, please expose it to me first."

The following week, on that particular Sunday, Clifton joined our besties and I at church. After church, we would usually go grab a bite to eat, so we went to have breakfast at IHOP. While we were sitting at the table, my sister-in-love, his baby sister, was talking about an event that she had attended the night before. It was the retirement party of a mutual friend, who happened to have also been Clifton's former boss from Los Angeles. Clifton had retired from that job, so he did not attend the party, but I noticed as the conversation commenced, he chimed in more than a few times. He seemed to know more details than he should, especially since he hadn't attended. As you can imagine, I tried not to interject just to see what else would be shared from his side of the table. I was sitting directly across from him. My "spidey sense" began to tingle, and I was simultaneously thinking, *How did he know that?* Now that everyone was distracted by the story she was telling, she paused to mention that she had the program in her purse. The topflight female that I was asked her to "let me see it." As I was looking through the program, I ended up at a list of names on the back. My eyes zeroed in on one name in particular, "Tammy Willis." All of a sudden, the flood gates opened up, and my brain started ticking in overdrive. My mind was flooded with thoughts and moments. Pauses and questions suddenly began forming into a devastating truth. That was the same name associated with the phone number that flooded my phone bill. Dang! I knew who Tammy was. She worked with Clifton. I also knew who she was because when her son was in preschool, he attended the school I worked at. Dang! He was always dropped off by his father. I would see her on occasion here and there when she picked up her son sometimes. He lived with his father.

I immediately nudged sis, and I said, "Come with me to the bathroom!" I whispered, "I have to tell you something." Clifton was looking at me from his side of the table. Was he on to me? He looked a little strange. I jumped up from the table, and I said, "I'll be back. I need to make a phone call to my mother." I fast-walked out of the restaurant and ran when I got outside to call my best friend, Teresa. None of the standard greetings our salutations were necessary. This was an urgent call. I thought I had solved the case, and I needed to go over my mental notes with someone. I told her, "I know who the telephone number belongs to."

She said, "I know. You said the name was Tammy something, right?" She was being calm, talking me down in case I had forgotten I already told her the person's name was Tammy. This is one of the reasons I loved her, and she was a best friend. She was usually my voice of reason, my calm during some of my storms. She knew all my business. So now I began adjusting my tone to help her help me feel better.

I said, "Yes, no! She is the Tammy that used to work with Clifton!" This Tammy was not even on my radar because she was a baby, a kid. She was seventeen years younger than Clifton and only two years older than our daughter.

I got myself together and went back into the restaurant. I tried my best not to show the turmoil that I was internally experiencing. Clifton knows me. He began to watch my every move. I was mindful. I could tell he was trying to read me by gauging my actions, my tone, and my words. They already finished breakfast when I made it back to the table, which was fine because I had pretty much lost my appetite. We finished up with the bill and got all our to-go bags situated. I whispered to Sis, "Ride home with me because I need to talk to you, like right now!" I felt like I was about to explode inside.

She agreed to ride with me. Once in the car, I explained the phone bill incident to her. I began to tell her about the telephone numbers on the bill and how he reacted and how he said it was just one of his clients. I told her that the number belonged to "Tammy" from his job. I told her that I was "going to do a little more investigating to see what else I could find out." If there was more to this, because now I believe that Clifton and Tammy were messing around, I would get to the bottom of it. My questions would soon be answered. I immediately went home, and I started looking at our phone records. This was in November of 2010. I got on the phone and made a call to Verizon Wireless and proceeded to order our phone records. I requested those cellular phone records for as far back as I could go. I ordered the records all the way back to 2000 and paid for the next day's delivery.

The box arrived. I had a strategy. I wanted to work through all those pages smartly so that I could visually reference the information easily. As I began to go through the pages, I would highlight every time I found Tammy's cell and home numbers. Then it hit me. I realized that she was also calling from the job number. I then went back to the beginning and started highlighting those work number instances in a different color. Needless to say, I was devastated after it became more and more clear. There had been a lot of calls made between the two of them over a substantial period. Now that is the main part that really got me. Clifton and I, along with my sister- and brother-in-love, had traveled all over this world within the last few years. According to what I could see, Clifton and Tammy were communicating while we were on vacation, all our vacations.

Whether we were in Tahiti, Fiji, or on a cruise somewhere in the Caribbean, they were still in contact with each other. I had ordered the phone records from as far back as 2000, and from what I could tell, they started calling each other in 2003. That happened to be around the same time I was planning the first "Heart of a Woman" event. I could not shake the sentiment that during all this time, over all these years, I was sharing my body with another and vice versa. I was in a threesome because, during a lot of our marriage, he was in a parallel relationship.

There were calls exchanged on our anniversary, my birthday, and any and every special occasion on which we shared our undying love. She was there too.

I am not crazy, and I am definitely no pushover. Clifton came home every night. On occasion, he still had late nights that he had to work. He was at that gym though, right? After highlighting five years' worth of phone record evidence, I would watch a little television. I was ironically drawn to and entertained by a lot of the "forensic files" styled genre that included the investigative television shows. I would watch *48 Hours* and *Snapped*. I had even become partial to a few of the court shows that came on in the afternoon. I guess I didn't know then, but I know now. I was being prepared for battle. I was starting to see that my rose-colored glasses were a little foggy.

I've learned that you need as much evidence as possible to prove your case. The search began. I was consumed by my thoughts. The mitigated Gaul of "Him! Her!" searching through drawers and regularly searching all his pockets became my tiptoe pass time. Of course, I got the outfits that were hanging up in the closet, the old and new. Yes, the laundry basket was checked daily. I went through his car, and I began to find what I was seeking. The things that used to be considered random suddenly became pieces to a bigger puzzle. I started finding all kinds of little pieces of paper or business cards, apparently collected while on our travels. All of them had her phone number written on it. It seemed as if Clifton couldn't remember her number because he was constantly writing it down on something, making sure he would have it, I presume. It took me about two days, but now I had collected enough evidence.

I made reservations that night for Clifton and me to check in at the Embassy Suites. Since I had watched the shows, I knew that I needed to let somebody know my whereabouts. I was being safe just in case something happened to me. I called my bestie and my sis-in-love and explained to them how I was going to confront Clifton. I had already called Clifton to find out what time he would be home and what time he had to be at that gym. He told me that he would only have a client appointment that next morning. I packed a few things for him and myself for an overnight stay at the suites.

As soon as he came home, I met him at the door. I just told him that we were going to go spend some time together for the evening. I drove my car in case something went down, I wanted to make sure I had a way home. Clifton rode with me in my car, and we went to Tom's, a fast-food drive-through that we frequent often. He was hungry, so we went to get him a large shrimp dinner and a large size drink. I guess you could call it the last supper. I never told him exactly where we were going, but we were headed to the hotel. As we engaged in small talk, nothing significant, I decided to ask him a question or two. I felt like we were disconnected, not "us." I proceeded to ask, "Do you know how much I love you?"

He said, "Yes!"

We finally arrived at the hotel, and I went to check in. After we got to the room, Clifton said that he needed to go get ice to fill the ice bucket. I found that strange because he had never done that before. We have stayed in a lot of places. Never have we been concerned about getting ice.

I began to get undressed and waited for him to return. Eventually, it dawned on me, "It sure is taking him a long time to get some ice." Then it hit me. It was more than likely calling Tammy to tell her that he would not be able to talk to her that night because we were together. At that moment, I jumped up and put my clothes on. Not today! I was going to get to the bottom of this. As I was opening the door to the room on my way out to go find him, he was at the door, getting ready to enter the room.

He asked me, "Where were you going?"

I told him, "To look for you. You were taking so long!"

He came into the room and put the ice bucket down. He never even put the ice in his drink. We both undressed and got in the bed. I laid my head down on his chest, and again, I asked him, "Do you know how much I love you?"

His response was simply "Yes!"

To that, I said, "Remember when you told me about the young lady that was one of your clients and how you were doing some kind of work with her sister?"

He said, "Yeah!"

I said, "Oh, okay." Now Clifton's phone happened to be plugged into the wall on my side of the bed at that time. I got up out of bed, walked over to his phone, and called Tammy's number. He had previously said that the number belonged to Linda, Tammy's sister. Tammy answered the phone.

She said, "Hello!"

I said, "Is this Tammy?"

She said, "Who is this?"

I said, "This is Tina, Clifton's wife." She hung up the phone.

Clifton jumped up out of bed. He moved like the bed was on fire. The first thing out of his mouth was "Take me home! Take me home!"

I said, "I thought the number belonged to Linda and not Tammy?"

He was pissed. He just kept ranting, "Take me home! Take me home!"

I told him, "Okay, hold on, hold on. Let me get dressed." He proceeded to storm out the hotel room door. After I put my clothes on, I walked downstairs out to the car. He wasn't there. Then I decided to just go ahead and check out. I told the lady, "I'm going to have to check out right now."

She said, "Why?"

I said, "I asked my husband a question that I guess, he apparently didn't want to answer."

She began to apologize and express the sentiments that the front counter help always spews. "I am so sorry. You have already checked in, and the room is paid for. I'll keep it open for you in case you want to come back."

By the time I got back outside to the car, Clifton was standing there. He must have forgotten that I had my keys. He didn't know what to do. He started walking around the car onto the parking lot in silence. I got in the car, so he turned around, walked back, and he got in too. We rode home in silence.

I did ask him, "Do you want to let me know what's going on?" He didn't say a word. I said, "Okay!" When we got to the house, I pulled in the driveway, and I said, "Are you ready to answer my question?" To give him a preview of my thoughts, I reminded him, "You said the number belonged to Linda, but Tammy answered the phone. Why is that? Why is Linda's phone being answered by Tammy?"

He got out of my car and never said a word. He went into the house, and I drove off. I went back to the hotel since I paid for the night. I slept there until the next morning.

Apparently, my son woke up early that morning or in the middle of the night, noticing I wasn't home. He asked Clifton, "Where's mom?" Clifton didn't really know where I was, so he just lied and said I was at his mother's house. That, of course, did not make sense to my child. Why would his mother need to spend the night over his grandma's house? I came back home the following morning. When I arrived, Clifton was still there. He had an early appointment that morning at six, but he did not make it. When I got home, I went straight to the computer and checked the phone records. Bingo! I was right. Clifton had called Tammy during the time he was supposed to be filling up the ice bucket at the Embassy Suites. I also noticed that he had been on the phone with his friend Anthony for about an hour too. I assume he was telling him what was going on with us.

I went up to the room to confront Clifton. He was just sitting there. I said what I said. He said what he said. We went back and forth like this until I knew that he was beginning to lie. That is the worst thing anyone can do to me, and that is to lie—when you lie to me about something that I am telling you I already know. Now I felt disrespected. I began to show him the phone bills and all the pieces of paper that I had collected with her number on it. He did not know what to do at this point. He literally just got up and left the house. I figured if he did not respect me enough to answer my questions, then I could get my answers from her.

Of course, I did. I went to her house. I do not know why. I did not think it out either. She was not there, or she was just choosing not to answer the door. So I proceeded to the job. She worked where he used to work at one point. It was the same place I had been going to pay the water bill for our house. When I walked in, she must have seen me and immediately went to the back. I waited in line until I got to the font of the counter, and I asked, "Is Tammy Willis here?"

The young lady up front said, "Oh! She is not here, ma'am." I knew that she was there though. So to avoid a scene, I decided to just go. I could not believe that this was my reality.

I waited for Clifton to return home. As soon as he walked through the door, I confronted him again. Again, he denied it. Then he said, "I will take care of it. Just let me handle it. Don't go up to the job anymore!" Clearly, she had already scooped him and told him that I had been up there. He said, "The guys in the warehouse called me and said they saw you, and they were asking me what you were doing up there." Now that didn't even sound right. The guys from the warehouse called! Really? I was in line to pay for my water bill. What could they have been talking about? They didn't practice that part of the lie obviously. I was in rare form. I felt a heat rise up inside of me, and I was relentless. Clifton could not turn his body or his head without me being right there in his face asking questions. I am not the same me I used to be, so I think I handled it well. Nevertheless, I guess after he talked to Anthony, they came up with a plan. They decided he needed to leave. He wanted to distance himself from me for a minute. He was going to go live in one of Anthony's mobile homes. I said, "Fine!"

Chapter 11

A New Beginning with Better Understanding

WE WENT BACK and forth, and he kept saying that nothing was going on with him and Tammy. One day, he came home and simply said, "Whatever we need to do, I will do." My husband got on his knees, and he said, "I don't want you to divorce me. It wasn't what you thought. But whatever we need to do, if we need to go to counseling, we can."

The way he got me was by turning my faith in God against me. He had been speaking to my in-loves, his sister, her husband, and his mom about his plight. They reminded him that I was a woman of God, and if he asked me for my forgiveness, as his wife, I would. Hearing this, I was stunned. I knew about forgiveness, and I am a woman that is strong in my faith. I thought, *Okay, if this had been me, if I had done to him what he was doing to me, if I messed up, would he give me another chance?* My number one goal in life has always been to live to please God. My second goal was to always be a godly wife, especially because I had an unsaved husband. My prayers were that he would eventually, one day, surrender himself unto God.

We mutually decided to try counseling. At this point, he had been living with Anthony for about two months. Every week, in front of the counselor, he would ask, "When can I come home?" I was still angry, so I was not ready yet. I was so disappointed. I did not deserve this. I was so hurt and upset. I was always present, pleasant, and an approachable wife. I made efforts to be sure that I kept my "Ts" crossed and my "Is" dotted in my marriage. I kept a clean house, prepared dinner, and our children were taken care of. Even his needs, mentally or physically, I happily did my part. I took care of the finances. I helped him out with his parents. Whatever they needed, I represented our household with my support. I handled everything. His primary responsibility was his training business. Thinking to relieve him of anything extraneous, I allowed it. I, too, had my businesses in event planning and decorating. I was also actively and faithfully working in the ministry, all while working full-time. In thirty-seven years, I have never "had a headache." One thing I do know is he could never say that I wasn't always available to and for him as my husband. What he did choose to say while we were in a counseling session was "When you were working and planning the Heart of a Woman event, I decided to spend some time at the gym." I would soon learn that apparently, not only was Tammy at the job, but she was also at the gym. I still agreed to continue counseling.

I pronounced to him that the love I have for him in my heart was still there. I needed Clifton to know that it was going to take some time to rebuild my trust, but on January 10, he came back home. We had attended the counseling sessions for a couple of months when he told me, "I want us to have a new beginning with a better understanding."

Since we were clear that an understanding between us was necessary, I, too, had a proclamation. I told Clifton, "I need a bigger house!" I also told him, now knowing what I didn't know before, "I don't like the fact that I have to pass the street where Tammy lives on my way home from work."

As you know, whenever I made up my mind that it was time to move, we were moving. I found my new home, and we moved in.

Things felt consistent and began to feel purposeful. Clifton even agreed to start coming to church at least twice a month. I had other requests for him too. I simply said, "No more trips to Vegas with the guys." He agreed. I wanted to say, "No more out-of-town runs with Anthony." At least not until I could trust him. I didn't want to affect his money though, so I thought about it, and I decided he could go with Anthony, but only up to a certain point until I felt I could trust him again. Vegas was a hard no though. He agreed. Clifton was working his business. The children were thriving and growing up, so they were doing their own thing. My mother still lived with us. I did more Heart of Woman events, and I was doing parties. Now that we had gotten settled in, we began to travel again, even more than before, with our travel buddies, his sister and her husband. Oh, and for the record, as for all those little pieces of paper with Tammy's number and pages and pages of phone bills, once I showed everything to him, he took them, and he claimed he burned all of it. It felt symbolic of our new beginning. Plus, I knew that if I kept holding on to them, I would never be able to let it go so that we could truly start over. That chapter was now closed as far as I was concerned, and we were "happily ever after," so I thought.

This is how the "not so ever after" began. Clifton started spending more time away from home, and he was at the gym even more. His hours were getting longer and later, and that was a problem. This became a regular argument because we were spending less time together. As time went by, we discussed him making changes to his schedule on the weekends. The goal was for us to spend more time together. The habit became him working later and later though. We went through this for a while, and I wasn't happy. Sometimes, I would attend our church's women's and wives empowerment class. I wanted to see if maybe there was something I was doing wrong in my marriage. I had been praying for this man for I don't know how many years that he would desire to be saved and live a saved lifestyle. Meanwhile, I was constantly trying to work on trusting him again because I was disturbed by the hours he was working at night, and I was not happy at all. Every time we discussed it, a fight ensued. I grew tired of fighting all the time. I just wanted some peace. So I would pray and tell God that I didn't know what to do. Sometimes, I would just back down because, in every other area of my marriage, I was happy and content. I lived in my dream home, and I traveled. I had my church, I had my family, I had my friends, I loved my job, and I had my event planning business on the side. Most of my dreams had come to fruition.

One thing I will say about Clifton, he was a good provider. I mean, I can honestly say that Clifton brought his paycheck home for thirty-seven years, the money he made by working at the gym or driving trucks. With that money, he was able to do as he pleased. He was always a gentleman, opening doors for me our entire marriage. If I needed to talk to him, he was respectful. He would turn the television down and give me his full attention. So my only complaint was the lack of time he had for me. I wanted to hang out sometimes and fellowship with family and friends together if he could have just changed his hours at that gym! I didn't think that I was asking too much. I enjoyed him and wanted to spend time with him. It changed in 2018. My "happily" again was happy no more. I could sense that Clifton was beginning to pull away a little bit again. We used to be very intimate. We always slept under each other. That began to change toward the later part of the year. We had gone on a Mediterranean cruise with my in-loves in late October. During the day, we were the perfect couple, affectionate, and engaged. Clifton and I were good. Everything felt real and seemed normal. When it came to the evening hours, his truth was revealed. Instead of our usual connectedness, he would just turn over when we went to bed. I thought, *Okay*, for a while. Then he started making excuses. He said he was having issues with a sciatic nerve, and his medication was affecting him. I thought, *Okay*, for a while. I tried to speak to him about it. I suggested that he plan to make an appointment with his doctor to see if he would prescribe something else. Now, I was thinking, *We've been intimate all this time, and you just can't pull the plug just like that.* So why was he avoiding me on this trip?

The cruise ship was beautiful. My in-loves had gotten off the ship for a snorkeling excursion. This was the only time over the many years that we traveled together that we would split as couples because they liked to snorkel. Clifton did not know how to swim, and I was too chicken to try it again. Whenever we traveled, we would take an island or city tour. Clifton and I loved to see where the natives lived. We were on one of those tours, and the trip had a stop that was at a mall. I was in the store shopping, of course. Every place I went, I would always be sure to purchase a sarong from that particular country or island. Clifton always bought a baseball cap and a T-shirt. We collected coffee mugs as a part of his collection from traveling around the world.

I must have come out of the store too soon because Clifton wasn't right outside. He had gone over to the pharmacy. I didn't pay it much attention because I know he said what he said about his sciatic nerve giving him problems on and off. He was always taking supplements and vitamins and stuff. He was buying some pills. I didn't know what they were, so I asked him, "What are those?" He told me, but I hadn't heard of it. He said it was something that would help relieve his back pain. I was thinking, *Okay! Tonight would be the night that things could get back on track, and we could be intimate.* We arrived back on the cruise ship and met up for dinner with my in-loves. After dinner, we came back into the room. Now it was supposed to be "us" time. I was looking forward to spending time with my husband. I was thinking, *Okay, he got the pills to take away the pain from his back. Let me freshen up because we are about to get busy.* Not! Do you know he had the nerve to tell me, "I am so full. I ate way too much at dinner. Let's do this in the morning."

Here we go. Well, I knew that was not going to happen because we had an excursion planned the next morning. We already had to get to breakfast extra early. We had to be off the ship by seven thirty that morning. At that time though, I looked at him and told myself, "I am not begging anybody to sleep with me! Goodnight!" I rolled over and went to sleep. We continued the rest of the cruise and returned home. Something just didn't sit right with me when we got home. I know my husband. I was thinking, *Something is going on. I'm not quite sure who or what.* About two weeks later, November 3, 2018, when I got home from Bible study that night, Clifton told me, "Anthony called, and he needs me to go make a run out of state." He said, "I'll be back late Sunday night."

I said, "Okay." I was planning a wedding in Laguna Hills, a couple of hours away, that weekend. That was fine with me. It was Sunday afternoon, and for some reason, when I got home, the house was empty. No one was home. Clifton hadn't made it back in town yet. Sometimes, I saw visions. I was wide awake, and I could see a scene play out in my mind out of nowhere. I was home by myself, and I was sitting on the couch, watching TV. All of a sudden, I looked over at my front door, and I visualized a highway patrol officer coming to my door. The officer rang my doorbell, and I got up and opened the door. He said, "Ma'am, I'm sorry to inform you that there has been a fatal accident." Then he said, "There has been a death, ma'am." Then he simply hung his head down.

The first thing out of my mouth, for some reason, I asked the officer, "Was he by himself?"

The officer said, "No, ma'am, he wasn't!"

I said, "Where did the accident happen?"

He told me it happened somewhere out of town.

I said, "Thank you," shut the door, and I sat back down on the couch. I immediately prayed. I said, "God, whatever this is, I don't know what it is. I don't know what this means, but, God, I need you to hold my hand." I began to pray for Clifton and my children because I was not sure what the dream meant, other than death.

I continued to watch TV. Normally, Clifton would have gotten home around one or two in the morning on the following Monday after he had traveled with Anthony. Clifton would call and sort of check in, giving me an update or time line, and I would usually wait up for him. But on this particular trip, he did not call me, and I did not know when he would be arriving. It was Monday morning, November 5, 2018. I got up and got ready for work then headed to the job. I will never forget that day. I was at the corner of Twentieth Street West and Rancho Vista Boulevard, sitting at the signal light. I started remembering and reflecting on the vision I had. All I could do was hold my hand up in the air, and again I said, "God, whatever this is, guard my heart, hold my hand, and don't let me go. Give me peace, Lord." I made it to work, and I still had not heard from Clifton. I was busy at work that day, so as time ticked on, I didn't have time to realize that he had not called me yet.

It was around three twenty-one in the afternoon, and I was in my office. Parents were sitting in the foyer, waiting to pick up their children at three forty-five. I got off of work at 4:00 p.m. So my area was full. I was multitasking. I had a parent standing at my counter when Clifton called. He said, "Hey!" That's different. We don't usually "Hey" each other. But I responded in turn, and I, too, said, "Hey!"

Then suddenly, he asked, "Are you happy?"

I said, "Yes and no. No, because of the hours you are keeping and the fact that we aren't spending much time together."

He then proceeded to tell me, "Well, I'm not happy. I'm almost sixty, and I want to be happy."

I proceeded to say, "Can we talk about this when I get home because I'm at work, and I have people looking down my mouth." He agreed. Before hanging up, I said, "Oh, by the way, this didn't catch me off guard because the Holy Spirit showed me that something was coming down the pipeline. I just didn't know what it would be, so this does not surprise me."

To that, he said, "I'm going to be home late tonight."

I said, "Okay, what about Tuesday night?" He agreed. I said, "Okay, we'll sit down, and we'll talk Tuesday night." The conversation ended because I hung up the phone. Driving home that day, I couldn't help but review everything in my mind. I was replaying the last couple of days, reminding myself of the red flags. I could not believe what had just happened.

To my surprise, when I got home, Clifton was there. I did not expect to see him since he said he would be late. I went upstairs to his man cave. He was just watching TV. I spoke, I said, "Hello." Then I went straight to the garage to begin putting up my inventory from the wedding I did on that Saturday. A few minutes later, Clifton came into the garage, and he stood behind me. He had this distraught look on his face. There was a darkness in his eyes and a distortion in his mouth like he was in anguish. He looked like someone had just died. He was pacing back and forth. He had a look that I had never seen before. I asked him if he was okay. He was acting like he was looking for something. He just said no, he was fine, then he turned around and walked out. I guessed he went back upstairs to watch TV. I continued to put my inventory up. It took me a minute, so I thought he had left the house because earlier, he did say he was coming home late that night. I thought maybe he was going back out. About an hour later, I went upstairs, and he appeared from nowhere. He immediately began following me as I walked toward our bedroom. He said, "I came home to talk to you, and you are outside messing with that stuff."

I said, "Clifton, you said we were talking on Tuesday. I didn't know you were staying!"

He repeated himself, but this time, he said it in an angry tone, "You're out there messing with that stuff, and I came home to talk to you!"

I again said, "Clifton, all you had to say was I came home so we can talk tonight, but you didn't. So how was I supposed to know?" We proceeded into the bedroom, and we closed the door. He went toward the bed to sit down, and I said, "No, let's go over into the prayer room." My mother was downstairs, watching TV, and the family room was directly under our bedroom. Honestly, I didn't know what to expect. I didn't know if we were getting ready to fight or if there would be a tussle. You know I still have another side, and I knew we were about due for a little turbulence anyway.

Instead of the stereotypical domestic situation, which I am sure I would not have been blamed for, I opposed fighting with my fist. I was in warfare though, so I wanted to be in my prayer room for the battle. We sat down, and the first thing I asked him was if we could pray. He agreed. I prayed, and I asked God to keep us in peace and to cover us through this valley. I said, "God, I'm not sure what's going on, but if you would, please lead and guide us." Then I asked Clifton to hold on a minute so that I could go get a pen and a piece of paper. I wanted to write down everything he needed to say to me. "I don't want to put words in your mouth, and I don't want no mis-understanding and no confusion." He sat there, too, and watched me prance myself into my bedroom. I grabbed a yellow tablet and ink pen. I then sat down beside him, crossing my legs, and said, "Now you can begin to talk to me." Here is what he said. Remember, I was going by my notes, so I was not putting words in his mouth.

He began by saying, "I am not happy, and I want to travel more."

I said, "Clifton, why are you not happy?"

He said, "I do not know."

I said, "Well, if you don't know, I don't know." I told him that honestly. No one will be able to fill that void but God. At that time, he was fifty-eight.

He said, "I am almost sixty, and I want to be happy."

I said, "We travel out of the country at least twice a year. How many people do you know do that?"

He said, "Well, I want to travel more." I decided to take that opportunity to remind him, "If you were home on the weekends more, then maybe we could do some more traveling." That, of course, caused an argument. Then he started venting. He said he didn't care anything about our house, and he never wanted the patio I had built. Again, he kept saying he wanted to travel more. He didn't like going to events with me, and he didn't want to move any more boxes for me. That threw me off a little because he only helped me four times out of thirty-seven years. Please do the math. We were not talking basic birthday party help though. My events were a workout. That should not have been a problem for a personal trainer looking out for his wife.

It seemed as if Clifton realized during our conversation that I was listening to him, and I was not arguing with him. I was not trying to fight. I have to say I, too, was surprised at how calm I was. I think he thought we would so that he would have a reason to go stomping out the door.

I could have been speculating that, but no, I was right. He came up with another way to get out of the house that night. He jumped up and started acting like he was having a breakdown. He began to say he was going crazy and that he was confused, and he didn't know what to do. He said, "I just need to leave!" It was crazy to me how he jumped up and started saying these things. I wasn't sure if it was because we were sitting in my prayer room. You know, when darkness needs to flee from the light. I was getting irritated by his antics, as I was thinking, *It's after nine at night. Where are you going?* I asked him, "Are you going to a hotel or Anthony's?" I just knew that the last time we had a similar episode, and he walked out the door, that is where he went. I said, "You know how ironic it is that the last time you left, it was around this same time of year, November."

He said, "I don't know where I'm going. I'm just confused. I just got to go. I'll call you tomorrow!" He picked up his pillow off the bed and walked out the door. Yes, I said he only took his pillow. Be reminded, he had just got back in town from being on a trip with Anthony, supposedly. I think he had already preplanned to leave, and instead of being out of town with Anthony, he had been with Tammy. I assumed that he probably told her that he was going to let me know that he was leaving. I figured all this out later. I was done. I went to bed. I asked God to guard my heart and give me peace.

He didn't call the next day. A couple of days later, I called him because I needed to know what we were doing. We talked about some things, and he wasn't making sense. I still didn't feel clear as to what he wanted, so I suggested that we try counseling again. He was acting like he was struggling internally, trying to decide what he wanted. I knew that something had him distracted. I was willing to try it again because I thought it worked the last time. He agreed, and I found a counselor that we had previously gone to in the past. Little did I know, at that time, he was still or had started up again, with Tammy. We had gone to a few sessions, and he had one recurring theme. His issue was the time I took on the Heart of a Woman events. He said he didn't like it when he had to pack up or unload the trucks. He said how he told me to hire people to help me load and unload then reload the trucks when I did my events. He had a point I could admit, but I needed him to understand the cost would eat into my profits. I would need someone for eight to twelve hours for each event. Anyway, I started getting more and more frustrated with him because he was making that out to be the reason. He was betraying our marriage. I was so frustrated, angry, and mad at him because he wasn't being honest and truthful. I just wanted to knock his block off. Instead, I would go to God and pray. I said, "Okay, God, I need you to help me right about now." It was like somebody had already made up their mind, but they were just going through the motions. The counselor wanted us to do date night because his goal was to try to get Clifton back into the house. Half the time, Clifton would not show up, or he would say he'll get back to me. We didn't follow through on the homework either since he never made the time to meet up with me. I was just like, "What are we doing?" I continued to ask God to just give me peace and guard my heart as we walked through this valley.

It was now near the end of March, and the counselor wanted us to sit down and discuss various topics since the date night and homework method weren't working, to see if our marriage was salvageable. He kept showing me though that he was no longer interested in "us." I didn't chase after him either. I told him and the counselor that something is wrong with this picture. I had been calling him, trying to stay connected. It became more and more clear that he didn't want my attention. I knew that I loved him with my whole heart, but I told both of them, "I am not chasing no man, nor am I trying to keep someone that does not want to be kept." My Bible said, "He who finds a wife finds a good thing and obtains favor from the Lord!" It hurt me when Clifton said to me in one of our conversations once that he knew that he and I didn't spend enough time together and that he was mad at himself. It caused him to have anger and bitterness toward me. He said that his heart had been hardened toward me, and he needed to get away from me. Allegedly, his heart was getting softer since he wasn't with me. That hurt me to my core.

One day, after finally tracking him down, I was able to get him to agree to go to the park so that we could do as the counselor wanted us to do. We both were supposed to write down some of the things that we needed to discuss. The main topic of discussion was if we were going to get back together or if we were going to go ahead and separate. Honestly, Clifton was already showing me this was not what he wanted based on his actions. I left the ball in his court. I was just saying that if this marriage was a priority, then we would have done what the counselor had been suggesting much earlier. I knew that I would be fine, and I knew that I was not going to beg anybody to be with me. Seriously, if you didn't want to play with me anymore, okay. I'll just take my toys, and I'll move on. But I still needed to know what we were doing. I was not going to allow him to keep leaving me hanging, knowing the whole time that he had already moved on. He was already living like he was single, doing whatever he wanted to do. Now, remember, he was out of the house. He picked me up, and we went to the park. We had Enrique pray for us before we left so things would go peacefully. What caught me off guard was when Clifton said, "I already know what I want to say." I was thinking, *Who have you been talking to because all this time, you can't seem to tell me what's really going on?* Of course, I came ready to listen.

I had my yellow tablet and pin, and I had written all these pages down. I wanted to be sure I said everything I needed to say. As I said, I had every intention to record what he said. I had been watching *48 Hours, Forensic Files*, and the court shows, so I knew how taking notes was relevant. He started the conversation by saying that he knew that we loved each other, but we were not in love. I had to correct him on that. I said, "Well, that is from your perspective because I still love you." He felt the need to tell me again that he didn't care anything about the house. We refinanced it, and I added on a patio with the money. He wanted to travel with that money and do some other things. He kept reiterating that he wasn't happy, but he couldn't or wouldn't tell me why he wasn't happy. I asked him if he was going through a mental pause. He looked at me and said, "What is that?"

I just said, "Never mind." I figured it was worthless trying to explain, so I didn't. He said he felt like everything he wanted always fell on deaf ears. He mentioned that the last two years, 2017 and 2018, were not a loving time for him. He felt that we were better off as friends instead of husband and wife.

I said, "Okay, so are you saying you want to do a legal separation, or are you talking about getting a divorce?" He said he wanted a divorce. I said, "Fine, but you are going to pay for it!"

Now it was my turn to go over my notes with him. I pulled out the yellow notepad, and I began to read him his rights. I read him up and down, backward and forward. I told him about himself too, the good, the bad, and his ugly. I broke it down to him about what I felt toward him as a father, a husband, and his role or lack thereof in this marriage. I did thank him for bringing home his paycheck for thirty=seven years. That was the one thing about him that he did consistently, and I could count on him in that regard. For that fact alone, I said, "Thank you!" We finished going over my grievances. I said everything I wanted to say, and I was spent. I then said, "Okay, can we go to 31 Flavors to get some ice cream?"

I know this caught him off guard. He was confused. I guess he was anticipating me crying and screaming with regret that it was "over, over!" Again, I'm not going to beg anybody to play and stay with me if they want to leave. There were no hard feelings because sometimes, people change their minds. I just believe there is a way to do things. This was not a simple phone conversation. I wanted to see him see me see him when he told me it is over. He took me to get ice cream before he took me back home. Once we got in the car, he started driving in a different direction than home. You know I watch my shows, so my spidey sense started kicking in, and I was feeling a little defensive, in case I needed to pay close attention. I had a crazy thought too, *Is this man about to drive me to the middle of nowhere? We are way out here in this desert.* I was feeling super dramatic. I thought, *What if he tried to kill me and leave me out here instead of dropping me off?* I turned to him and said, "Where are you taking me?"

He said, "I'm taking you home."

I said, "Oh no, excuse me, I don't live this way. I live the other way. You need to turn around!" Of course, he did. I think he was distracted by everything that was going on.

I started telling him that we would need to discuss who was going to keep what and how we were going to do things. I let him know that I was still going to need his help financially.

Now I was going to have to retire and go get another job. I was still trying to work back in Aerospace again so that I could have two incomes. I told him I wanted to keep my home since it is my dream home or at least until I build another one. This home gave me peace. It was full of love. This was the house where our families would gather, mine and his, and I wasn't going to let it go. It was after that day that I said, "God, I don't know what this is?" I found myself in the closet again by the way. This is where I go when I want complete focus and a quiet moment with my Father.

God, whatever this is, please expose it to me. Clifton would still come over to the house on his lunch break, in between clients, while I was at work. He also left his paycheck to pay the mortgage. Then we were separated and headed toward divorce. He still had a key. Time had gone on, and on this particular day, I received an email. Now just to set the scene, I took care of all the finances. Everything Clifton had, I set up. Every email, every password, every account, everything came to me.

I was at work, and my boss was in my office when I got the email. Right before this, I had been the victim of an identity thief. A person had gotten access to my credit cards. When I received the email, I assumed that someone had gotten access again. I felt a little distraught initially because he took forever to get all the fraudulent charges taken care of. I had finally gotten everything changed and had alerts added to all my accounts. Now this.

I got an email from Carnival Cruise Line, so I opened it up. It said, "You have eighty-nine days before sailing." This was the first of June. On April 1, Clifton decided that we were going to go ahead and go our separate ways. That was the day that we met in the park. We no longer went to counseling after that either. Imagine my surprise to find out that Clifton and Tammy were going on a cruise to the Mexican Riviera. It was completely paid for already too. So you know, I did the math. I jumped out of my seat, and my boss said, "What?"

I said, "Oh my god! Oh my god!" I told her, "It's a good day, but it's a bad thing."

She said, "What's wrong?"

I said, "Look! Clifton and Tammy are going on a cruise."

She said, "Who is Tammy?" I told her who she was because her son was going to her school when he was three. He might have been four. I reminded her that he lived with his dad at the time, and she would pick him up sometimes.

I said it was a good day. My boss asked me, "How could it be a good day if it's a bad thing?"

I summed it up for her real quick. I said, "I can see that my husband is having an affair." I said it was a good day. I asked God to reveal to me what was going on, and He did. Now my boss knew about Clifton and me and our divorce proceedings. Needless to say, I didn't say anything to Clifton about my knowledge of this trip, especially since we were separated. I held onto the information. Their cruise was scheduled for September.

Clifton continued to lie about different things concerning his whereabouts. Like for instance, he and Anthony were supposed to be in Mexico working. My daughter-in-love told me that her mother saw him in Kohl's Department Store. Not only did she see him and call him by name, but they also had an entire conversation. She asked him, "Where's Tina?"

He said, "Church!"

She then told him to tell me that she said, "Hello." He was in the store with another woman. He lied to his mother. He told her he could not come and assist her with his ninety-seven-year-old dad. Yet there he was, at Kohl's Department Store.

My daughter-in-love's mother called her and told her that she had just seen Clifton at Kohl's Department Store. Knowing what was going on within our family, she called to tell me. I called Clifton, who would have been no more than fifteen minutes away, to ask him to come to show me how to work the lawn mower. He stopped cutting the grass, so I needed his assistance. He said, "I'm in Mexico." Anything I said, he began to just lie about everything. Even things he did not have to lie about, he did. I began to do my homework and pay attention differently. You know, like my show, *48 Hours*. I was on the case, and I found out the truth, the whole truth, and nothing but the truth! So help him, God.

I shifted gears, and I called him, asking him to come over. I wanted us to sit down and write everything out. I wanted to discuss how we were going to take care of things moving forward. He needed to be in agreement. I needed time because I was still trying to get a new job. I truly needed him to help me financially, at least until the divorce was final. I didn't let him know that I knew about Tammy. I did tell him that God had revealed some things to me, that he had already moved on.

I told him exactly what I had concluded that all the "guy trips" to Las Vegas, the times he stayed in our time-share. I had the receipts. I had the receipts of every time he had checked in without me—those trips dated back to 2005. I also found out that he was making money renting out our time-share to his clients. I confronted him. I told him, "You might have gone somewhere, but you were not with who you were supposed to be with or who you said you would be with." He denied everything. I asked him about several things that I needed to discuss. I asked again, "Do you want to do a legal separation or a divorce?"

He said, "Divorce."

I told him how God had revealed to me that I would be going to the courthouse to file for divorce. From that point, I pulled out my yellow tablet, and we sat down, and we both signed what we had agreed on—what each of us was going to keep and who was going to take care of what.

The next day was July 24, 2019, the day of our thirty-seventh wedding anniversary. I went to the courthouse, proceeded up the stairs to the self-help center, and filed for divorce. I continued to ask God to keep me and to guard my heart. I needed to make it clear that I wanted him to never let me go. That was crazy.

Like we discussed, he paid the fees, but I only asked for half. I had spoken to one of my close girlfriends, Ellen, a couple of days before that. I told her that I was going to go out to dinner for my anniversary after I left the courthouse. She told me that she would take me out to dinner so I would not be by myself. We made arrangements for her to pick me up, and we went to this Italian restaurant in Palmdale. Our waiter led us toward the back of the restaurant. Once we got into the back room, there were about thirteen women seated there—my mom, my sister, my sister-in-love, my niece Kelly, my BFF, and so many very, very close friends of mine. Ellen had her sister-in-law decorate the room.

I was so surprised. The table was transformed with centerpiece settings, along with a candy bar decorated in peacocks. It was beautiful. I told them that peacocks meant a new beginning. I called it my "last anniversary" party. We had fun. I was so happy that day, even though I had just filed for divorce. I called Clifton to let him know that I had filed and that I would have my nephew serve him instead of embarrassing him and serving him at the gym. He told me that no, he couldn't meet him. Every opportunity after that, he flaked. He just started giving me the runaround. You are not going to believe what I did.

Since he did not want to do me right, I left the papers with his mother, and she served him when he came over that Sunday morning. You may be saying, "Wow! That was pretty low having his mother serve him." A girl had to do what a girl had to do. Later, when I spoke to Clifton, he told me that he would be staying in one of the mobile homes that Anthony owned. At the same time, I was still receiving emails. The latest email alerted me that Clifton had changed his mailing address for two credit cards to Tammy's address, her house. I have Tammy's address. It was just crazy. Some of my close friends and family kept telling me that Clifton was not living with Anthony. He had moved in with Tammy. I was trying to give him the benefit of the doubt. Maybe he was telling the truth. Maybe he was renting a room from Anthony. I found out according to the address in the email, she lived right behind my church, the church that I attended at least two to three times a week, the church where I was an active member, the church that I love, where I worked in the ministry, the church that I was faithful to. I could not believe it.

It was daylight savings time. I got to church early that day because of the time change. I'll never forget it. I was waiting to go teach a new member class. I arrived before anyone had gotten there. On Sundays, Clifton would go to his mom's to assist her with his dad. He helped her between eight and eight thirty in the morning. I figured I had extra time on my hands, so just to get myself out of my misery and because I knew where Clifton was for sure, I took a little drive. I parked on a side street across from an open field from Tammy's house. I could see the front door and the garage. I was getting ready to turn some music on because I figured I would be sitting for a few minutes. As soon as I found a station, the garage door opened. Clifton's car was parked inside her garage. I was in shock. I grabbed my phone because I wanted to take pictures to confront him. I had long nails, so instead of getting the shot, I kept hitting the selfie button about ten times. Instead of taking pictures of him, I ended up taking pictures of myself.

I opened the door, and I was going to get out, but then I didn't. I thought, *No! He's going to see me.* I didn't know what to do. I didn't know whether to drive across the field and run straight into him, pinning him into her garage. I had to think on my feet and think fast. I knew he was going to be pulling out, and I needed to confront him. So I jumped back in my car, and I sped around the corner. She lived on a cul-de-sac, so it was a dead-end street. I pulled over to a side street and waited for him to pass me. He passed me but didn't notice me. I made a U-turn to follow right behind him. We both turned out onto Twenty-Fifth Street East. I knew where he was supposed to be headed, and he should be making a right turn. I knew we would meet at the intersection at about the same time because I was headed toward the church, so I was going to make a left. I was thinking with that in mind. I was planning to blow my horn and call him, asking, "Where are you coming from this early on this side of town?" He was supposed to allegedly be living in Lancaster. We were in East Palmdale.

I was going to confront him and let him know that I had just seen him come from Tammy's house, but he moved from the right lane and then moved over to the left lane and ended up right in front of me. I was a little bit behind him because the signal light turned red, stopping him. As we were at the light, he looked in his side mirror, and he looked again. Then he looked up in his rearview mirror. I smiled and waved, then he waved. He saw me see him see me. The light turned to green, and he immediately sped off. I positioned myself, getting right behind him as if I was going to follow him. Not today though. I was coming up to the church, so I had to turn into the parking lot. I had a class to teach—no time for foolishness. Amazingly, I was able to teach my class and keep my composure. I just saw my husband pulling out of a woman's garage at eight in the morning. I knew 100 percent without a doubt that he had moved in with her. It had been confirmed.

Clifton made it to his parents' house right after that. I'm sure he wanted to tell his mom before I did. He ended up telling her that he was at Tammy's house because she was cooking him breakfast before he came over there. Why did he walk in the house telling his mother why he was at Tammy's house parked in the garage so early in the morning? At that point, his mother knew nothing about him possibly living there—unless he was guilty and was just trying to cover for himself. I came to the realization and accepted the fact that he was living there.

Now I was trying to get over that crazy shock. Never in my wildest dreams could I have imagined that I would see my husband, on four different occasions, pulling out of "her" garage at eight in the morning. We were not even divorced yet! I told myself, "Listen, girlfriend, this is your reality, so get yourself together." I can truly say I'm in position, and I have a purpose—even the times that I saw my husband coming out of that woman's house. Despite this, I was on my way to do preservice prayer and to teach new members class. God erased all that hurt and disappointment, and it didn't interfere with anything that I had to do. But when I walked up out of the church at the end of the service, the heat in my heart would rise up. I would talk to myself, and I got myself together. I continued with that process to get through it. No matter how agreeable I was though, he would still lie about everything.

Now the time had gone by, and the month of September had come. It was time for the trip. He already had some regular existing responsibilities. His obligation to help his mom on Sundays was supposed to be a consistent commitment. I gave everyone a discreet heads-up though, just in case. I told our families that he was going to lie because we already knew he was going on the cruise. The email was confirmed in June. He still didn't know that we knew. Of course, as predicted, he lied about his whereabouts. He told me, along with his sister and mother, that he had to go out of town with Anthony to Texas to pick up a mobile home. On the Friday that he was leaving to go on this cruise, this is what I did. I had received an important email regarding his cruise itinerary. I called him and left a message for him to call me because it was very important. He returned my call. I mentioned to him about the bad weather they were having in Texas, and he said yes, they were experiencing some bad weather. I told him Mexico was having bad weather too. I explained to him that per the email he had just gotten, the itinerary had changed for the cruise that he was going on, but they could still check in at 1:00 p.m. From that point, I began to tell him how I have known about the cruise for a while, and I had been getting all the emails regarding them.

Clifton had added Tammy to his credit cards at this point, and I had all the receipts. I took that opportunity, and I asked a question, "How are you going to be in Texas and Mexico at the same time?"

All he could say was "I can't talk now." My mission was accomplished. I told him to call me back, and he hung up the phone. I just wanted to let him know that he was now exposed. His lies were coming to light. I continued with my evening. I was busy. I was supposed to be setting up for a wedding. I received a phone call from my sister-in-love, Renee, that evening. She told me that she, along with her mom, had called Clifton and told him that he needed to call them back as soon as possible. They were trying to confirm him because they knew what I had already told them, that he and Tammy were going on a cruise. They told him he needed to call because their mom was hurt. She was upset because he lied to her and said he could not come to help her assist with his dad. He told her he had to go to Texas. They needed him to call them back. They wanted to hear it from him to clear up this mess. Well, needless to say, Clifton turned off his phone and did not return the call.

It was much later in the evening, around nine-ish, and I had just finished setting up the decorations for the wedding and reception. It was then that I realized Clifton had not called me back. I called him, but I just left a message because his phone went straight to voice mail. Then feeling a little messy, I called Tammy's phone and left a message for her regarding the change in their cruise itinerary. I left her a detailed message too. I told her that I had gotten all the emails for their trip. Before I hung up, I ended the call by telling her that she did not have to worry. I would not be calling her back because Clifton and I were getting a divorce. Then Clifton called me back.

For the record, I just knew that now he would not be able to lie about his whereabouts. I called Carnival Cruise Line the Friday before they returned and told them I needed to get some information to one of the passengers. The woman that answered the phone asked if it was an emergency. I said no, but it was very important. She asked for the name of the ship, the room number, and the two passengers' names. I gave her all the information that she needed. She then asked me who I was. I said, "I am Clifton's wife." She then asked me what message did I want to be relayed to the party. I told her, "Would you please tell Clifton to call his wife regarding his dad." A few minutes went by after I left the message, then the phone rang! It was Clifton returning my call. The first thing I said to myself was "Bingo!" Now lie your way out of this one. I told him that his mother wanted to know if he would still come over on Sunday to help with his dad. He responded but immediately hung up the phone. I laughed to myself, thinking, *I guess I just ruined his breakfast.*

When Clifton got back from the trip, I had a revealing conversation with him. I thought I was going to confront him, but you will not believe what came out of his mouth. I was floored. I could not believe it. He deserved some type of award for the best character played in a nonsupporting role. Are you ready? He told me that Tammy didn't sleep in his room with him. He didn't even know where she slept. I decided to play along since he was intending to insult my intelligence. I said to him, "Oh, so the cruise line put her name on your room reservation, authorizing her to use your credit card?" This man said they put her name on his room because the room had to have two people listed on it. At that point, I was done. The lies just kept going on and on. It was embarrassing.

As we were getting closer to the end of the divorce process, time went on, but the grocery list of lies continued. I was still in a good place though. I was getting comfortable in my new normal and embracing the beginning of my new journey. I continued to ask God to hold my hand and to guard my heart. It was not hard for me to adjust to the fact that Clifton was no longer home. He had always kept late hours anyway. I would just tell myself he was still at work, and then I would go on about my day or night. It was sad, but as I was going through it all, I was thinking, *I'm okay!* I was still as busy as ever. He was the only change. Remember, I already took care of the home, the finances, whatever the children needed, and I even took care of him along with his parents. He was the only thing I didn't have to take care of anymore. Actually, I do have to take the trash out now. I have to learn how to cut my grass and mop my floor too. I am a survivor though, so it's nothing.

Now that the divorce was final, honestly, I didn't hate Clifton, and never once have I harbored any bitterness toward him. However, I was very disappointed in him. I lost respect for him, and I had lost the comfort of trust. There were just too many unnecessary lies. I was okay with him, possibly changing his mind. Sometimes, people change their minds. People get divorced every day. My primary issue is I know that I deserve better, especially after having endured thirty-seven years of marriage. We were together for thirty-eight years. I know I was committed to the part where you say, "Till death do us part." I expected more from him. He could have been man enough to let me know that he and Tammy never actually stopped messing around. Even if they had just picked up where they left off with their relationship, he could have been straightforward. He could have said he wanted to be with her and not me. Instead, he lied to me. He lied to his children, to his parents, and to his family.

I took my toys, I took my children, I took my grandchildren, I even took Clifton's parents and his family, and I brought them with me. In other words, all the holidays we've had since Clifton and I separated, Christmas and Thanksgiving, are still at my house with my family and his family. His parents are still my parents, and I still go see them like always. His family and I still get together for special occasions. We check on each other. They love me and support me. I still get invited to family events instead of him. I think it is pretty sad, but because of all the lies, he burned a lot of bridges within his family. One Sunday, one of the women from the church and I had a quick chat. She said she wanted to talk to me. I told her that I was divorcing Clifton. She said she had something to tell me, but she never really wanted to say anything. She had met Clifton at our home when I was hosting a small party for the ladies. I guess at one point in the party, he had come downstairs to speak and welcome everyone to our home. She said the way he looked at all my guests, she could see that he had a whorish spirit. She recognized that in him because her father was the same way. He had a whorish spirit. I was floored. I just looked at her and walked away.

A couple of months before the divorce was final, I was visiting my in-loves, Mom and Dad. We were all on rotation. Every Thursday, I took them dinner and helped to put Dad to bed. Clifton's mom and I began to talk, and I told her that on New Year's Day, Clifton and I were supposed to meet up because I wanted closure before walking into the New Year. He, of course, wasn't available. He kept putting me off, so we spoke over the phone. Did I ask him if he and Tammy ever stopped seeing each other after the first time? Yes, I did. He said they were not together. I reminded him of all the receipts I had collected, which contradicted what he was currently saying. Still he said, "Yes, we stopped." He said Tammy came up to him in the gym and told him that she had heard that we were getting a divorce, and whatever he needed, she would be there.

We talked about why he lied about going out of town when our friend saw him at Kohl's Department Store with a woman. That brother told me that they thought that it was just Tammy that he was friends with. He had a few friends allegedly. There was another Black woman with braids. There was a Caucasian one and a Latina. Clearly, during our conversation, we had crossed over to have an understanding. He was talking, and I was listening. I told him he was really going to need some Viagra now. My mother-in-love and I were standing in the kitchen at the time we had this chat. Suddenly, she stopped in her tracks. She turned around and said to me, "Clifton had always had a whorish spirit." Those were the exact words the woman at the church said.

She said she thought that when he met me, that it was going to all go away, but it didn't. He told her when he met me how happy he was and he wanted to marry me. As a Christian woman, she thought that he would change his ways after we got married, but evidently. Then she looked right at me and told me, "You are free!" She told me I was free to move on and that I should walk in my freedom. I was in shock to hear that come out of her mouth. Of course, now I was thinking, *Why didn't she tell me about his whorish spirit after he messed up with Tammy the first time?* Then she threw another curveball at me when she told me that Clifton had cheated on his last girlfriend to be with me. It wasn't until recently that I learned they were engaged. He left her to marry me. I had no idea.

To hear all these truths about my husband after the fact, after thirty-eight years, I didn't know whether to cry, scream, or laugh. I was thinking, *She has been holding that information in for this long. She, too, is now free.* Once Pandora's box was opened, I found out information from other family members that confirmed his whorish spirit. A few people cleared up and confirmed a few areas of concern that I had regarding Tammy. It all came together—the pieces of the puzzles, the red flags that I had talked myself out of. Like they say, "If you follow your first mind, you can't go wrong." Well, I should have believed what was revealed the first time.

Now I continued to walk in my freedom. My "happily ever after" had come to an end with Clifton. My internal happiness continued to drive me forward. God had already planned my journey. By creating and writing the script for the "Heart of a Woman" and the "Learning to Love Yourself Even the More" events for seven years, I was being prepared for a time such as this. Not knowing then, during those times, that my heart was being guarded. I was able to enjoy the majority of my marriage sheltered from the darkness. I love me enough for the both of us, so I had already learned to love me. Because I created the workshop "Who's Loving You," I already learned how to not allow anyone to outlove me, loving me. Even though he pulled the rug from under me, I mean snatched it with no warning, I loved him with my whole heart. When he walked out, I still had some love to sustain me, and I was able to continue living my life. I was able to continue to laugh. I was able to continue to still have my peace. I was able to continue to still have my joy. I was able to continue to function and do what I needed to do.

I learned through all this that I don't have to act like, look like, nor do I have to smell like the hell that I've been through. In other words, just because you have been through the fire, you don't have to smell like smoke. I'm just saying. I bought a sign and placed it on a wreath over my door. It said, "It's so good to be home." Every time I walk through my front door, I read that sign because this was the home that I desired, and God granted me that desire. Every time I walk in the door, this is where love resides. This is where I meet my daddy, my spiritual daddy. He spends time with me, and He lets me know that He loves me. He continues to remind me of who I am to Him.

Some are probably asking, "Whatever happened to Clifton after the divorce?" Until this day, I never really found out what would make Clifton happy. Other than, he said he became unhappy when I created the Heart of a Woman event. He learned that he wanted to travel more, and he did not want to help unload boxes anymore when I had a big event. Clifton said he was now dating three to four women, including Tammy. I guess after all these years, all she had ever really been is a side-chick second place. She tried to remove me from the number one spot as his wife only to find out she would never be wifey. Like he told me, "I don't ever want to get married again." He said that he was not in a permanent relationship with any of the women, and he did not belong to anyone. Now I do have to say that he shocked me when he told me that one of the women was in her thirties, and she had a two-year-old. What! So she was younger than Tammy? Remember, Tammy was seventeen years younger than Clifton. At that point, I was done.

I guess as long as he's happy now, it's okay with me. But honestly, if you have to have that many women, then you are not happy. I am just saying. I truly believe he was going through a midlife crisis. But oh well. It is what it is. I was not trying to make somebody stay when he clearly needed to leave. I never want to get to a place of desperation that I am trying to force someone to stay with me. When their role has been fulfilled, then allow them to be released. Sometimes, you don't feel the weight of something you've been carrying until you feel the relief of the weight being released. I didn't realize how much I was carrying until it was lifted. We talk when we need to. But now he just feels like a family member to me, a part of the rotation.

Unfortunately, our children don't talk to their dad because of all the lies. Clifton seemingly just wants to sweep everything under the rug and ignore the elephant in the room. His decisions have affected all our lives. He had been not truthful and manipulating us for years.

Subsequently, he lost them and his two grandchildren. Maybe over time, that will change. I would hate it if, in the end, he wound up being just a lonely old man. My prayer is that it will all change between them, that they are able to rebuild a genuine relationship. As for me, I am in a good place. I am still trying to enjoy life to the fullest. I still plan to travel but just with my girls now. I am going to sit back and enjoy my retirement. Who knows, I am free, I may decide to do something else. If God sends the right man along, my heart is not closed off. I can truly say that even after being together for thirty-eight years, love did not fail. We did.

God is love, and He never fails. And it takes two to tango when you are dancing to the song of marriage. But I guarantee you, my next go-around, when "Mr. Frank" comes along, he's going to need to love God more than he loves me. Then he will know how to love me. He will know how to treat me. He will know how to honor and respect me. He will know that I belong to the Most High God and that I am a precious jewel. He will treasure me and my gifts because he has obtained favor from God by making me his wife. We will most definitely be equally yoked, making me his good thing. I found this quote on Facebook, and it was perfect. It said, "If life can remove someone you never dreamed of losing, it can replace them with someone you never dreamt of having. Through all this, in life, I have learned to be strong enough to let go and wise enough to wait for what I deserve." Now that right there, that is what I am talking about. Come on, Frank! As far as marriage, oh yeah, I see it in my future. I don't know when. I don't plan on looking for it either. When love knocks and if he meets the criteria in his relationship with God, then I will open the door and answer. But to be honest, with or without Frank, I will still have my *happily forever* after and then some.

Five promises that I held onto as I walked through my journey:

I made sure I put God first. I would always seek Him first, the kingdom of God and His righteousness. (Matthew 6:33)

I trusted and knew that God would provide and supply all of my needs. (Philippians 4:19)

I knew that God would never leave me nor forsake me. (Deuteronomy 31:6)

I held on to the peace of God that guarded my heart and mind. (Philippians 4:7)

I know without a shadow of a doubt, that God will give me a crown of beauty in exchange for my ashes. (Isaiah 61:3)

Chapter 12

Three Strikes and You Are Out

THREE STRIKES AND you are out. I was rejected for the third time. First, it was my father and his family that rejected me. I believe he never really had time to be a father. Well, at least not my father. I still don't understand how he could love somebody else's kids. Did he love me at all? I was his firstborn. His family pushed me to the curb a long time ago. I was never treated like a grandchild, especially compared to the others.

That man, I guess, I will call him my father, he remarried. If anyone ever cared to ask me, I would have said, "He loved her two children as his own." But what about me? I was his firstborn. So that was the first strike. I was rejected by that man. I thought that he should have loved me. He should have at least cared about me or acted like he cared that I existed. Scratch that! I know he should have loved me.

I didn't realize it back then, but all the baggage that I had collected through this journey, I held on to. I brought all that luggage into every relationship after that. Remembering who I am today, I celebrate these seasons. Here I am, telling you my side of it all in spite of the bondage.

The second rejection goes back to when I told you about the relationship that I had with Tony, my baby daddy. He was the forbidden love of my life. Yeah, I said it. We were too young and dysfunctional though. We were unequally yoked. There could never be a covenant between us. We agreed to agree. We both resolved to move on forever. He walked out of the door. At least he waited until I had the baby. The other two abortions that I endured were seemingly forgotten. He became "Mr. Rosalyn." The chick that I now know was her. Remember, he walked out the door on me, on us because of "her."

So add that piece to the matching set of luggage, complete with the brokenness and unspoken emotion that I had collected. It was so draining and counterproductive. The third and final strike though was him, Clifton. Thirty-seven years of my life, although realistically, I would only claim thirty-five of those years, we were living in marital bliss, or so I thought. Well, either way, I always envisioned it as blissful during those times. Until gradually, I couldn't put my finger on the who, what, when, or why because I stayed amazing and loving and affectionate!

In one moment, it just started feeling toxic. My marriage became the exact opposite of blissful. It was dark. I was in a void of confusion and uncertainty. Nevertheless, "Lord, I know to trust you over everything, seen and unseen! I am your baby girl, Lord! I need you to help me understand! Lord, what happened?"

This kind of rejection penetrates your spirit differently. It's beyond personal. It's biblical. This was a connection that I thought was my destiny, my tomorrow, my forever. Now what? How did I find myself here? Never in my wildest dreams could I have imagined that now at "go time," I would have to endure this type of pain. Clifton was my life, other than my children, my mother, and my family. No one could compare. No love could compare. No unconditional level of forgiveness could compare to what I thought we had. I never thought that I would be here. Not now. I was the next batter up to the "plate" called life. I was good at what I do. I was ready to make this home run hit. I expected a victory, only to end up striking out for the third time.

Did I see it coming? I'm not sure. There is always that moment where intuition kicks in and has you second-guessing certain red flags. You talk yourself out of it though because he would never. I had given all that I knew to give. Maybe, just maybe, I could have squeezed out a little more of my time and adoration, making sure that he always felt "special." I could be speculating though. He was the only one that knows what he really wanted and needed. Clearly, as far as he was concerned, his needs were not being met. Let me think about this, "What if I am wrong?" No! Scratch that. Delete that thought. He was the one that was wrong! We said, "For better or for worse," and all the stuff you are supposed to say in front of your loved ones and before God. We had a covenant. I signed paperwork.

He walked out of the door. When he walked out, it was behind the tail of a much younger woman. Let me put it in perspective to make sure I am not exaggerating. She was two years older than our daughter. Wow! Let me be clear. I am at the end of understanding, tolerance, and forgiveness. Enough is enough! I was in the middle of foolishness. It felt like déjà vu. "Really, Clifton, after all I have done for you? I stayed covering for you! Especially through a lot of your hidden ways! You know what I brought to the table! I was your wife! I always had your front, back, and side. I was supposed to be your rib." I took my vows to "love and to cherish" seriously. My love was sacred because I loved him. "Really, Clifton?" For me, this was the third and final strike. Game over, or so I thought.

So after I filed for divorce, I realized that the one that had shown up in my life a while ago was always the one that ultimately has my back. He was always around, and I knew it. I probably took advantage of that at times. We had a connection though. Even during the darkest times, I knew how to call. He was always there for me when I needed anything, whatever was on my list. You know how it goes, "It's me again. I need you!" He would say, "I am on my way, baby girl. I told you, you can always count on me!" No questions asked. He is always there. In a time of sorrow, He gives me peace. He makes all things better, especially during this time while I am enduring this storm. He has been my strength whenever I feel weak or just worn out. Then it happened. I remember when "He" asked me, "Do you love me?"

As I thought about what that meant, I decided to remove the mask. My past didn't matter. The things that I have been through, my faults, my scars, my wounds, my downfalls, and my mistakes, didn't matter. I was self-conscious about my insecurities and my secret fears. I just knew though I am in love, an agape love that surpasses all understanding and reason. "It is what it is," and this is real! This is better than I could have ever imagined.

I remember being told that I was loved while listening for the first time to "I Found Love," a song by BeBe and CeCe Winans. I was reconfirmed then because I knew what we have, this is special. He told me that I was fearfully and wonderfully made. There's a song He played for me, a song that I absolutely love by Bruno Mars called "I Love You Just the Way You Are." Now that's what I'm talking about. Just that right there, "What?" I realized I was being serenaded. This song triggered within me—an awareness that would soon define me. I needed some time and attention.

It was during this time, in that place, it was at that moment right there where I found peace. When I was confused and didn't know what to do or where to go, it was like a reminder. I had this epiphany that confirmed, those men did not define me. "I am enough!"

I still knew that I was loved. He makes me see His blue skies even bluer. They seem clearer and crisper, if that's possible. Like when you go on a fast and your senses become heightened? It is a blessing because now that the rain is gone, the sunsets on the horizon are seemingly more vibrant too, a horizon that appears to have been colored by an artist's brush—beautiful colors in different hues but in the same shades with slight variations of orange, red, and yellow. The colors seem to merge as one. To this day, I embrace my relationship with Him. We have a personal love, a bond that discloses all the details. We have an intimate understanding of one another. I will never forget the whisper in my ear when I was being told that I was loved from the foundation of the world. "What? Is it like that?" I thought, *He loves Him some me!* I am told daily, in a still soft voice, a whispered sentiment just for me. He loves me. Every morning, He kisses me as I rise. His breath is my life. Each day upon the new days dawning, when I open my eyes, the new mercies that I receive remind me. Because I am loved, I, too, am purposed.

His creations seem to envelop me, rocking me slowly, a renewed calm. Like the ocean, I am essential even to me now because He loves me. When a soft gust of wind passes by me now and then, I remember I am not alone. He is always present in my mind, so my thoughts turn into real-life smiles as I say, "Thank you! I love you too."

These words are not enough. How can you read a smile? Well, I am smiling from the core of my being with my whole heart. I know I am loved now, inside and out, the good and the bad, in spite of the "shoulda, coulda, wouldas." Nobody has ever loved me the way He loves me. Even though the men, the relationships, the betrayals, the other strikes, he didn't judge me or make me feel convicted by my journey. He stayed available but allowed me the time to make my own decisions. There was never any pressure. He was always just there just in case I needed to come calling for a fix. He is so special. Boldly, I can truly exclaim that I am contented and confirmed that this love needs to be a priority in my life.

He said when He found love, He found me. Yeah, me! He loves me enough to lay down His life for me. Now I am sure I am his favorite because He calls me "baby girl." That's right. I said it. I am my daddy's favorite. He allows me to just climb up in His arms spiritually, and He comforts me. He comforts me for as long as I need comforting. During these lows, these sad times, I imagine that I am laying my head down, right on His bosom. I am there, just dwelling under the shadow of His wing. Our relationship is customized and designed for me too. I love that the most. That's what I call love. Now I ask you, "What man in this life can love you like that?"

He told me a secret, and, of course, I believe Him. He said, "Out of everyone in the entire world, you are special. I know the number of hairs on your head. I knew you before you were in your mother's womb. I know why you are here on this journey."

"Yes, Lord!" I cried. "I trust you with my life and everything that is to come. Your will be done, Father!" Oh yeah, I'm a baby girl, but I am also known as the daughter of the Most High King, and He knows my name. You can call me Tina though. I'm just saying.

Chapter 13

The Pain, the Pitfall, the Platform

THE PAIN, THE pitfall, the platform is what God showed me. The pain consisted of darkness, disappointments, anger and betrayal, rejection, and hurt. These were the things that I had to walk through. These were the things I learned to suppress—the pitfalls that led me to one to many valleys, valleys and hills that I had to endure in order to be freed from my past. I have come to realize that the very things that I have had to overcome, my yesterdays, now I used as a platform. I am a vessel to be used by my maker. I want my steps to be ordered so that through me, His will may be done.

You may be asking, "How did I take all the trauma from my past and use it as a platform?" I was able to pull from a place deep within. I placed it right on the table and defined its space in my life from that point forward. With my testimony and my truth, I was able to speak about how I turned my pain around, resulting in positive outcomes. This was how I began my restoration and healing process so that I could do the same for other women. The first restorative platform that I created was called the Heart of a Woman. When this vision came to pass, initially, I had no way of knowing what was to come. My platform evolved when the Heart of a Woman was born.

The Heart of a Woman was an event that was designed to celebrate women. My mother and I would invite women to our event in order to celebrate *them*. One of our life's missions is to build up the self-esteem of women to encourage, honor, appreciate, applaud, and respect them for who they are. We like to love on them by showering them with token gifts of love, showing them their self-worth—just our way of reminding them that they are someone special in life. We wanted to create an environment of wholeness and wellness for the women. We strive to instill positive scenarios to help encourage and develop life-changing results.

The women came from different demographics and were on different levels economically and spiritually, from all types of backgrounds and age groups. Some of the women came from brokenness and had been abused and misused. We rolled out the red carpet for their arrival. I was inspired to create skits and motivational readings that relayed a message visually and emotionally. The celebration was an interactive environment. A theme for the event was to show the women that they should be crowned as the queens they were. So at every celebration, we crowned their beauty by presenting them with their own rhinestone tiara. We let them know that royalty was their middle name. We showed them that they were precious jewels and that they were as beautiful as any butterfly. We reminded them that when God looked at them, He only saw a reflection of an angel that was coming from within them. We introduced them to their internal light by showing them that they were the beauty of a rose.

We spoke words of encouragement, letting them know that they were a gift that should be celebrated each and every day. They were told that they were one in a million. Positive affirmations were presented as seeds planted to help them learn to love themselves even more. They were given mirrors to look upon their reflection so that they may realize how to accept and acknowledge themselves for who they are.

We started off with fifty women being celebrated in 2003. There were seventy-seven different women in 2004. In 2006, 225 women were celebrated. In 2007, we realized this was becoming our dreams manifested. We celebrated 450 women. Then in 2008, there were 650 women celebrated. In 2009, we celebrated 500 women. In 2016, we celebrated 500 women. God used this platform for seven years.

Loving Yourself Even theMore

Another platform that was birthed from the pain and the pitfall was a workshop that I taught for seven years called "Loving Yourself Even the More."

These workshops were held at a domestic violence shelter. Men and women were invited to come together, giving us the opportunity to let them know that they weren't bound by their current situation. Regardless of their past, they could move forward. They could start all over again. Each participant was given a pen so that they could rewrite their story. This time, in this instance, they could write their ending.

They were also asked to write love letters to themselves. They were given a new set of symbolic keys. These keys were meant to show them how to unlock some doors. For sure, a lot of them needed to lock some doors. We even discussed those doors that needed to be closed and locked. Positive seeds of affirmation were also planted and spoken over them. Mirrors were given to them so that they could look at themselves. They needed to be shown how to accept and acknowledge themselves for who they were. With that being said, we would share other motivational readings to empower and encourage them to move forward from their trauma. The scars and wounds that they had suppressed from their past were acknowledged.

The Princess Masterpiece

Then there was the trip to Kenya, Africa, the birthing place of my next platform. It was here that the Princess Masterpiece platform was born, the blessing that I didn't see coming, little me, Tina. I was celebrating forty young girls varying between the ages of seven to seventeen. This was another life-changing moment that God allowed me during this life's journey. These girls were sold into marriage at a young age. Through God's grace and mercy, they were rescued.

I taught them how to love themselves, no matter what. They were worthy of love. As far as who they were, they deserved love. They needed to be told. So I did. I let them know how God sees them. I placed tiara crowns upon their heads and told them that their beauty had been crowned. I explained to them that royalty was their middle name. I reminded a few but shared with most that they were like precious jewels that should be treasured. I said this as I adorned their necks with a single strand of pearls. I proclaimed into their lives that they were fearfully and wonderfully made. I wanted to plant the seed that each one of them was different and yet a masterpiece. They were like a designer's original. They were daughters of the Most High King. If nothing else, I wanted to embed in their hearts for them to be who they were regardless of what anyone else said or thought. They were to rise up in their silence. They needed to be told that they have the power to move mountains. Be ye not afraid and have hope and faith.

God chose to allow passage through another open door. He allowed me another moment to be used as a vessel. I was blessed to do a second workshop. He sent me to work with a church, hosting young girls between the ages of eight to seventeen. This time, I established a similar platform for five weeks. The Lord ordered my steps right here in the states. As in Kenya, the Lord manifested a blessing. In each "moment" I was afforded, both ended in unforgettable ceremonies and celebrations.

Who's Loving You?

As I was walking through my divorce, God gave me a fourth platform called Who's Loving You. This was another five-week workshop since I do workshops now. This one was at my church. This was a workshop to teach women how to love themselves. Most of them had been enduring the ultimate betrayal. They had the carpet pulled from up under them.

I reminded them that they needed to love themselves, that the person that they sold out their truth for, the one they thought they were madly in love with. Him. If "Him" chose to walk out the door because life happens, and it happened. Have they learned how to press forward, even if their love tank has been left empty? That their dreams can still come true. We discussed tools that they could use once the devastation kicks in. If they could understand how important it is that they learn to love who they are when life happens and love walks out the door, they would then know that situation was not the sum of them. They still had God's love to sustain themselves.

But there were topics that were covered in order for them to get to a place of loving themselves. They were instructed to remove the mask. Don't be guilty of identity theft. That was first on the agenda. Letting go of unforgiveness and bitterness was next in line. Once they removed some things from their past, they began to open up and speak to embracing and loving themselves. She loves me, she loves me not was also covered in the workshop. Each woman was asked to write a love letter to herself. After every session, we had a toast to celebrate who they were. The last workshop was all about them. We all embraced and just enjoyed the loving atmosphere full of beautiful people that were accepting who they were with or without any validation from anyone.

So now looking back over yesterday, as I said earlier, God used all the pain, the darkness, the hurt, the disappointments, the trials, and the tribulations to walk through a pitfall, a pitfall that took me to a very low place. In spite of this, He impregnated me with a platform that would allow me a stepping-stone. Through it all and nevertheless, sometimes, when we're going through a pitfall, we don't realize that what we are going through is not just for us. The million-dollar question that has crossed my mind, and if you are honest with you, you too have likely spoken it or thought about it, "Why me?" and "How much more do I have to take?"

Guess what I would come to find his response was? Why not you?

God already knows how much you and I can bear. You have been assigned your assignment long before it arrives at your door. Because what the enemy means for evil, God can turn that thing around for your good. Then we can turn that around again. He will position us so that we can be a blessing, all while offering encouragement to someone else. They can then do the same.

The pain that I felt from yesterday, the "pitfall" that I had found myself in, I climbed out. I rose up. He brought forth through me a platform that allowed me to be a blessing, encouraging many upon many. I was thinking back over everything that has been on my journey thus far, again, the good, the bad, and the ugly. I had an epiphany. A key necessity of the delivery process is the birth. In order to be impregnated with life in your womb, it must first be predestined. The platforms that I was given were predestined. When He chose me to become, he placed in me, in my womb, the moments that were to come through these platforms. He knew all these things before I even had a journey on this earth. My prayer has been for many years, "God, use me as a tool, a vessel, an instrument." I prayed that He would use little me, Tina, for His glory. He did, and He is.

Chapter 14

The Still Waters

I WAS IN a place that I needed clarity, and I was seeking some direction for my life. I made a big girl move. I accepted my reality and decided to face my truth. This divorce was at the end of my tunnel. The light within me allowed me to feel a sense of peace. I wanted confirmation though. I was ending a covenant, and it meant a lot to me that my Father guided me through the process, every step of the way. I wanted to know that I was still dwelling under the shadow of the Almighty.

On October 5, 2019, it was a Friday afternoon, and I had just arrived in Greeley, Colorado. I had planned a surprise visit to attend a fundraising banquet. This fundraiser was for Saruni International, an organization that rescues young girls that are sold into marriage in Kenya. I had the opportunity to visit Kenya, along with some of the sponsors that were connected to the organization. We spent two weeks together, and we fell in love. The movement and the cause are so necessary. To have been a part of making a difference was a goal accomplished. We formed a friendship, a spiritual bond that still exists to this day. I wanted to share how we met.

I had taken a girl's trip to Los Cabos, Mexico. From camel rides to beaches, volcanos to ruins, the trip was amazing as always. There is something about the synergy of like minds around water. On all our trips, we would always be sure to commune in and/or around a pool or body of water. On this day, the crew and I were in the swimming pool, hanging out toward the end of our trip. We were really enjoying one another's company. There were fourteen of us in the group. We laughed and high-fived our way through several shared memories.

Toward the end of the day, there was a couple that had entered the pool. You could tell they were cool because they were comfortable adding to our conversation. As the pool time conversation took a turn for more serious topics, the couple began to tell us about the Saruni Organization. I was taken aback when they invited us to come to Kenya. They suggested that there was an opportunity to be a mentor for the girls. To be so comfortable speaking to perfect strangers about helping in a way that speaks to me was timely.

Before they got out of the pool to catch the early dinner buffet, they asked us to pray about it. We said that we would, and the group of ladies I was with on this trip, I knew we would. We all have so much in common. I like that we share some of the same things in common. We will laugh together, cry together, play together, and most importantly, pray together.

Our visit to the pool came to an end, but before they left, we asked them their names, and she said Tina and Mark. I could not believe it—what a coincidence. We had the same name. It felt like confirmation. Our easy connection felt purposed. It's like when you hit it off with a total stranger in the nail shop or salon. You chat through the entire appointment, and then you find out you have the same birth date. We exchanged contact information on our phones. I put a star on their contact information. Plus, her name was Tina.

The trip was amazing. As I got settled back into my normal hustle and bustle, I would think of them fondly and often. I love it when the Lord uses me as a vessel to do His will. It is like being chosen for a special assignment because you are the right piece to the puzzle. Your inclusion makes it all come together. Of course, until it all unfolds, you don't always know the assignment.

After a couple of months, they reached out to me. They wanted to talk to me about taking the trip to Kenya. As we chatted, I found out that they were supposed to be staying in the hotel next door to where we stayed while in Mexico. Their hotel was under renovation, and they just so happened to have been moved to our hotel. Believe it or not, Tina told me when they decided to go to the pool area earlier in the day. They were at the pool on the other side of the property. There were some young people in that pool, and they were being a little rowdy and rambunctious. Clearly, the drinks had been flowing on that side of the hotel. They decided to check out the other pool, which happened to be the pool that the girls and I were relaxing in. The way He weaves together these moments that He allows me always surprises me. It was our last night there when Tina and Mark had just arrived. It was a divine connection for the two Tinas to meet in a swimming pool in Mexico.

My trip to Kenya was life-changing. It felt purposed. It was such a beautiful place, full of beautiful people. Kenya has always been on my bucket list. I am so grateful that I have had the opportunity to check this moment off the list. I met the rest of the group that was in partnership with the organization. They were from all over, Colorado, Florida, and California, of course.

Now here I am in Colorado, on a visit to surprise everyone and attend the fundraiser dinner. I was excited and looking forward to the chance to just steal away from everything. I had made arrangements with one of the young ladies in the group once I knew I would be able to go. We discussed the details of my arrival, and she had made plans for me to stay with her during my visit.

My plane touched down in Colorado on October 5, 2019. It was a Friday, and Maggie was picking me up from the airport. When she picked me up, she told me that I would be staying at her parents' home instead of her apartment, as we discussed. She failed to mention that she had a dog that was the size of a pony, and her place was small. Of course, I was fine with that. I thought that it was kind of her to be so gracious. I was okay with that, assuming that she would be there with me though. Let me remind you, this was my first time in Colorado, and I had never met nor seen her parents before.

Maggie was cool, and I loved her, so I just assumed that I would love her parents too. We made it to their house. We entered through the unlocked back door. I was coming from a city in California, and we would never leave our back door unlocked this way. Maggie said, "Oh! We leave the back door unlocked from time to time."

I told her, "I am from California. We lock our doors." She laughed so hard, she snorted. Clearly, she thought I was joking. I told her, "When we leave this room, can you please make sure to lock every door downstairs?"

As we toured the house, I realized that Maggie's parents weren't home. That threw me off a little since we had gotten there that evening.

Maggie didn't stay overnight at the house with me either. We ended our tour before she left in a room upstairs that was decorated with an old-fashioned comforter on the bed. There was a white rocking chair that sat next to a tall floor mirror that leaned up against the wall. It reminded me of a room that would be in a country bed and breakfast. After Maggie helped me bring my luggage in, she told me that she would see me the next afternoon around 2:30 p.m. As a footnote, she reminded me to be ready for the banquet and volunteered that we needed to be there early. I had no idea what I was walking into. When she walked out that door, of course, I locked it. Since now, I was home alone.

The next time I looked out the window, it was pitch dark. I didn't see any light, especially no streetlights, like at home in California. I became a little nervous. To be honest, I was scared. I called both my mom and my spiritual mom as I walked through the house, turning the lights on. They had me laughing and distracted. I still told both of them that I was sleeping with the lights on.

It was so quiet in that house. I could hear that a fly had entered the room. He must have been coming home for the night because I didn't hear one more buzz the entire evening. I decided to pray, just in case. I said, "Okay, God, it is just You and me. I need You to keep my mind right about now." I laid my bible out so I could keep the Word right next to me. I was serious.

After what seemed like forever, with my senses on high alert, listening and watching the silence most of the night, thank goodness I was finally able to fall asleep. I did wake up once or twice for inevitable reasons. I stole a peek at the outside, and it was still pitch-black dark. I could not wait for the morning to arrive as I tiptoed at top speed back into bed.

When I woke up, there was a sliver of sun that kissed my eyelids open. I sighed a sigh of relief. I made it. The morning had arrived. I said my prayers, thanking Him for letting me make it through the night with no hurt, harm, or danger crossing my path. I felt like I had made it through the longest night ever. I got myself together and walked down the long main hallway with dark wood paneling that embraced the walls. At the end of the hallway, there was a large wooden spiral staircase with a banister and stairs that were the same color as the wood paneling.

I found the other bathroom as I made my way downstairs. It was beautifully decorated in a country theme. I mean, it was beautiful. I looked at everything and took a few mental notes. There were a couple of ideas I saw that would work for my guest bathroom. In addition to that, I was silently hoping and praying that Maggie's parents had made it back home. I washed my hands and checked the mirror once more.

The house was empty. It was just me and the sound of silence. The air was so still, no breezes or movement, just stillness. On my way to the kitchen, I had to pass through a couple of rooms to get there. All the downstairs rooms had the same wood paneling on the walls. The entire home was just lovely. I could feel and see that there was love there. There were family photos of the adult children and what seemed to be all the grandchildren too. Even the pictures had a country theme. There were pictures taken in fields of wheat or some kind of grain. It could have been a cornfield. After absorbing all the decor, there was no question that it was a country-styled home. I think it like the *Little House on the Prairie*, but this was a big house. As I walked through the house in the light of day, I noticed things that I didn't notice before. There were no televisions. This stood out because as I walked through the family room, I noticed that there was no TV in that room either. I finally made it inside the kitchen, and it was adorable. I instantly felt comfortable and at home. Maggie told me to help myself to anything, so I decided to look for something to eat. I checked the refrigerator and pantry. I knew that Susan, another friend, would be picking me up for lunch soon. I figured a little nibble would do because I knew I could hold out until Susan got there.

I took my snack outside with me onto the porch. It was so tranquil and peaceful. The smell of the country air caused me to inhale deeply. I felt led to do a little fake yoga-like stretch to match my mood. Birds were feeding on a feeder outside of my bedroom window. I noticed when I woke up this morning. I saw that window from where I was standing. Looking up, I realized how big the house was. It was Saturday morning, and I found myself on that morning, climbing up, and I mean up, onto a full-size swinging bed hanging from the ceiling of a screened-in patio. The property was surrounded by flourishing mature trees that bordered the beautiful two-story brick country-style home.

As I took it all in, I began to meditate. Eventually, I could only hear the songs that the birds were chirping. I began to think about how "everything that has breath shall praise the Lord." The leaves were blowing soft, and you could slightly feel the gentle touch of the wind. I knew He was with me. I could feel his presence around me. He began whispering to me, "You thought you were coming out here to surprise everyone at a banquet." It was true. The way I received the message, I knew it was intended for me to realize, this was a moment for me. He wanted to talk to me, and He brought me all this way to slow me down so that I could listen uninterrupted. Sometimes, He's possessive and wants all my attention. He told me I needed to be in a place of stillness, a place where I could only hear His voice. He said there are no TVs here, nothing to take the place of the stillness of my voice. I removed you from where you were to a place of tranquility where all the chatter has ceased, and the frequency of my voice is magnified.

I said, "Here am I, Lord. It's just You and me." It's like He removed everything and everybody around me. I was glad I brought my journal downstairs with me. After sitting up in the swinging bed writing in my journal, I decided to go out and explore. So I left the patio, and there were trees and acres of horses directly in front of me. All I could see was his creation, and it was beautiful. Everything looked so nourished and green. You could still feel the dampness in the morning air. There were large pine trees everywhere and what looked like sprawling green pastures.

I walked across the wide driveway to a second large building. Apparently, it was the man cave of Maggie's dad. Adjacent to that was an attached garage for all his large motor toys and cars. Directly behind the large building was a ravine. It seemed to surround the entire property. You could tell that when it rained, the water would flow in a certain direction, connecting one side of the property to a separate area. I had no way of truly knowing how many acres I was standing on. I just kept walking. I followed the flow of the water as it went in the direction that I felt led to go. I was at peace as I realized I was being led beside still waters.

As I continued to walk, I began to listen as my Father spoke to me. The silence and stillness in the air were unbelievable. It's like when you see an expansive body of water that looks as clear as glass without even a ripple.

I began to speak Psalm 23, "The Lord is my shepherd and I shall not want. He makes me lie down in green pastures. He leads me beside still waters. He restores my soul. He leads me in the path of righteousness for His name's sake. Even though I walk through the valley of the shadow of death, I will fear no evil, for you are with me; your rod and your staff, they comfort me. You prepare a table before me in the presence of my enemies; you anoint my head with oil; my cup runneth over. Surely goodness and mercy shall follow me all the days of my life, and I shall dwell in the house of the Lord forever."

Like the scripture stated, I felt like, though I was walking through this darkness, it felt like I was right in the midst of "the shadow of death." That is exactly what my divorce felt like. My financial foundation was now on shaky ground. I never had any fear though. I knew that I had a favor. I asked God the day that Clifton walked out that door on November 5, 2018, to hold my hand and to never let go. I asked Him to guard my heart. I knew that His rod and staff were comforting me. I am not sure when, but I knew that He would prepare a table in the presence of my enemy. If I don't know anything else, that is "anything that the enemy meant for evil, my God can turn that thing around for my good!" I knew this was so for me especially. I am His baby girl, and I belong to Him.

The neighbors across the gravel road were stretched out far apart. There was still no sound other than the birds singing and chirping their praises. I just kept walking. Before I knew it, I had walked down quite a way, so I decided I better turn around and headed back. When I arrived back at the house, I walked up and into the front of the yard. The front of the house was as big as the other side of the yard. Where I was, there was a white wooden picket fence. This fence was expansive. It, too, lined the property. That main street was a couple of feet away, but you still couldn't hear the sound of any passing cars. A blanket of peace enveloped me. I knew I was going to be just fine.

I started smiling because I thought about looking forward to what was to come. Again, I had no idea what I was walking into. But God already had it orchestrated for His purpose and His glory. The scripture in Psalm 46:10 said, "Be still, and know that I am God." It had manifested. This scripture had come to pass. It had definitely and clearly lifted from the pages and right here looking me eye to eye. It was unavoidable and right there in my face. The voice of God was saying, "Be still and just know." That is all he wanted me to do. Just know that He had me. The rest would fall into place.

By this time, I made it back into the house, and I was preparing for Susan to pick me up for lunch. I felt as though my joy had been restored. I knew God was still holding my hand and walking through this with me. I felt that He put me in that place called Greeley, Colorado, where He carved out a time and place for He and I to reacquaint. He wanted to direct my path. I felt like I was resting in Him and that I could return to California with an assurance that all is well. I felt a calmness down deep in my soul that words cannot explain. But I knew my heavenly Father gave me a tangible confirmation that day.

After lunch, we came back to the house so we could get ready for the banquet that night. We had a great time. We just enjoyed each other's company. We spoke about our family, our previous trip to Kenya, and so on. It was good to get out of the house. I was look-ing forward to the evening. As planned, we arrived at the hall a little early to take care of a few last-minute details and instructions for the banquet. When we got there, I stood inside, waiting to surprise Tina and Mark once they got there. When they arrived, I was stand-ing there dressed in a beautiful African gown and coordinated head wrap. I watched from across the room. It was clear that they had no idea it was me. Finally, they started heading in my direction, shaking the obligatory hand and blowing cheek-to-cheek air kisses along the way. They had no idea who I was as they got closer, clearly in route to greet me, introduce themselves, and welcome me to their beautiful event.

Wait, let me clarify something. Over the two days that I had been in the fine city of Greeley, I was the only chocolate-flavored person I'd seen. Okay, maybe there were two. So at the event, I stood out. The royal blue and gold gown that I was adorned in was a cul-tural showstopper in its authenticity. Once our eyes locked and it registered who I was, the shock was all over their faces. They said I felt familiar, but they didn't think of me officially because why would I be in Greely when I live all the way in California. Once they real-ized it was me, we hugged and cried. It was a priceless moment in the middle of the ballroom foyer.

My surprising them threw them off a bit. They took a moment to recover. I had heard a lot about the banquet, and it was amazing. I was so glad that I was able to experience it. I was able to finally meet Maggie's parents. They were at the event with Maggie's siblings and spouses too. I knew who they were. I was staying at the family's home. It was so much fun fellowshipping with everyone.

When the evening came to a close, I rode with Maggie back to her parents' house. It had been a long day, and I was more than ready to call it a night.

We chatted about my day, and I explained to her my still water experience and the encounter that I had with God. She had a few follow-up questions as I segued into why she had left me at the house alone for the entire day. I was grateful! I did tease her though, laugh-ing at how I prayed my way through the night, having been in that big house all by myself. I mentioned how I thought we were both staying at her parents' house together, especially because they were not home. I laughed it off, of course, but low-key. I was very serious. It all worked out in the end, so there were no complaints. She reiterated how she was unable to have me at her apartment because her dog was, in fact, as big as a pony. When I saw the dog later on during my trip, I instantly felt better. She was not exaggerating. Her response was "I don't know. I guess it was a God thing." I acknowledged and accepted her final statement. It most certainly was a God thing. The Lord knew the plans He had for me.

I had a restful evening. The silence was the perfect backdrop for my dreams yet to come. When I woke up Sunday morning, I realized I was here at this place during this time, seeking to hear from God. He allowed me the clarity I needed. He helped me understand what steps to take and which direction to go and what purpose I was to serve. He gave me an assignment. You, oh God, are such a loving and merciful God. You always take care of me. You allowed me something that I didn't know I needed. You gave me the opportunity to still away. You love me enough to set the perfect atmosphere to hear your voice, another chance to dwell in a secret place under the shadow of your wings. You are the Almighty.

I came down for breakfast. I still could not believe they let me, this African American woman, whom they only heard about through their daughter, stay overnight in their home unaccompanied. They trusted me enough to be alone in their home. I was sincerely humble and appreciative. I know I am cool, but they took a leap of faith and trusted me unseen. I felt respected, and I was humbled.

As Maggie's parents and I began to talk, of course, they wanted to know more. Their questions rolled off the tongue, "What did I do? Where was I from in California?" It always tickles me when people regard California as if it has some special power, a mystical state in our country. As the conversation continued, I felt the need to tell them about the divorce I was going through after they mentioned they would keep me in their prayers.

As we smiled across the table having breakfast, there was a knock at the side door. It was the early part of the morning. Who could that be? I wasn't dressed yet. A bouquet of fresh flowers was being delivered. Well, that was refreshing. It was more than just a bouquet. It was a beautifully appointed sentiment that was welcomed and timely. I knew to be reminded that all things mean something. I reflected on the creation of the flowers and the significance of how the smell of them was so present. They changed the mood of the room.

We cleaned up what was left from breakfast, finished dressing, and headed to church. Maggie was going to meet us there. The other confirmation, the sermon was "Being Still and Quieting the Noise." The pastor told us, "You can't hear from God unless you lean in when He whispers." Maggie's mom and I made eye contact at that very moment.

The church was really nice. I was not surprised. It was just like a present-day *Little House on the Prairie* with all of Maggie's sisters, their spouses, and children. They were all there. They were even sitting together. So clearly, they had their spot of the many pews in the huge church. They all sat together just like a loving, happy Christian family. Like their family pictures at the house promised, I was in the right place at the right time.

When church was over, as before, I felt encouraged and refreshed. It is comforting when you have a good, transparent talk with your Father, and He manifests the solution to what you prayed about in the most unexpected ways. He knows how to get you to listen if you have a relationship with him. I went back out to meet up with the Kenya mission crew, my extended family at this point. We all came together for my last day, which we spent memorializing our mission trip and how we all met. There was no patronizing or code-switching. I was so comfortable. I didn't stay out long though because the next morning, my visit would come to an end. I was heading back to California in the morning, wiser, stronger, and better. Won't He do it?

After I felt settled on the plane, California bound, mind you, I had to get buckled in and listen to the emergency exit presentation. I always listened just in case they have discovered a more enhanced and efficient way to conduct the existing standard operating procedure. It is the same on all airlines and has been for years. The plane ride home was smooth. I felt so clear in my purpose, and I felt excited about the assignment. The clouds in the sky seemed crisper and more vibrant, too, as the sun was reflecting its rays across His chosen clouds. It was a reminder that He was still God, and all I had to do was to be still and know.

Chapter 15

Tag, You're It

ON DECEMBER 27, 2019, I scheduled my annual physical exam with my primary physician. I took these appointments seriously, making sure to get a mammogram and Pap smear. Today's appointment was to get the referral from my doctor for the mammogram. I will never forget my visit that day. I had endured the standard preliminary triage questions, "Why was I there? When was the last time I had a menstrual cycle?" The nurse took my vital signs. I told her I would like to get a mammogram. She proceeded to tell me that Kaiser, my insurance, only authorized mammograms every two years. Likewise, I wouldn't be able to get a Pap smear. Those were every five years. I attempted to insist that I be able to get one today. She went on to say that the doctor would not approve of it. I was a year too early. For some reason, she had an attitude.

She continued with the task of taking my vital signs. She gathered her things when she finished and announced, "The doctor will be with you." Then she walked right out the door. Thankfully, I did not have to wait long. My doctor came in all cheerful. Of course, she was happy to see me. She asked me why I was there, and I told her the same thing, "I would like a mammogram and a Pap smear." She repeated the same thing the nurse said as if there was an "it is too early" script. She asked me if I was having any problems. I continued to repeat myself. I was adamant. She asked if I had multiple partners. I said no. At that particular time, Clifton, my ex-husband, and I were really in the final stages of the divorce. We were no longer together during that time. In vain, I was feeling confident because he was my only partner. It's been thirty-seven years. I hadn't been sleeping with anybody other than him. My doctor finally gave me the answer I needed to hear. She would give me a referral for a mammogram. I went directly to radiology to proceed to get a mammogram that day.

I received a letter about two weeks later that said I needed to come for another appointment because they spotted something. They wanted me to do a biopsy and get an ultrasound. Now it was January, and I went to the Kaiser Hospital in Panorama City. My mom, along with two close friends, drove down with me for moral support. Once the procedure took place, they said they would send the results. I was also told I would have to go back a week later to discuss the tests. Approximately one week later, I went to my appointment. I did not know that the appointment was with a surgeon. I should have caught on when I checked in with the receptionist though. There was a red flag or two. The girl at the counter had asked if I was there for surgery. I said no and explained that I was coming in for some test results. She just said, "Go to the third floor." Mom and I walked into the doctor's office on the third floor and waited for him to arrive.

The doctor walked in, introducing himself, and proceeded to take a seat. He wasted no time. He began to let me know what was going on and began showing me pictures. Then it happened. He started going over the report from my biopsy and the ultrasound. As he sat there in a comforting posture, he said it. I had stage 2 breast cancer, and it was 2.1 centimeters. Also, I had a surgery scheduled for me within the next two weeks to address it. It did not register right away. I heard the words, but I couldn't understand how that could be my truth. Those were words that I have heard before but never with a true understanding that they would be said to me ever, not in this lifetime.

As I was processing the plan that was undoubtedly routine in his reality, I was thinking, *Wait a minute, what is going on here? Why me? Am I missing something?* Here we go. "Tag! I'm it!" I just sat there as he continued to go on with his explanation, using technical terms and medical verbiage. He reiterated that we needed to get right into surgery, which, again, was already scheduled. He had me talk to the nurse to schedule my follow-up appointment. They left my mom and me alone, giving us a chance to grasp it all. We both had tears coming down our cheeks.

I was silent. The whole time I was thinking, *He just gave me the diagnosis, and they are ready to put me on the table.* I was thinking, *Tag, you are it. You are now playing this game of life, and you have just gained an alternate journey in an alternate universe because this can't be happening.* We left the appointment that day, loaded down with pamphlets and informative brochures. My doctor mentioned that on my next appointment, they wanted to do some other testing and find out something in relation to my genes and DNA.

Now I was thinking, *The ink on my divorce paperwork is not even dry yet, and now this? How much more will I have to take?* I thought walking through the divorce was my biggest blow before this happened. This has knocked the wind out of me and left me in a daze. After I returned home, I called my children, my family, and my close friends and told them what happened. I was totally shocked and in disarray. I thought I was healthy for the most part. I was never sick. I had never had the flu, not even headaches. I had plenty of sick time because I never call out sick. Besides that, nobody in my family had breast cancer. I had a couple of close friends that have endured it but nobody in my family.

They said after I have the surgery, for six weeks, I would have to undergo radiation treatments, five days a week. *Okay, I can do this. I will map it out.* I got myself together and planned for the surgery, and I organized my schedule for my upcoming medical leave. I braved through it all, but I will never forget the week before my surgery. I was sitting in the lunchroom at work when I got a call from the surgeon. He said he needed to tell me something. The test results that they just got back needed to be discussed with me right away. Immediately, I recognized that I needed to find someone to help me get through this call. I did not want to black out or lose it, especially because he said he had some bad news. I ran down the hallway at work and found my boss. I simply said, "I need you!" as I mouthed that "It's my surgeon," while pointing to the phone. I put my phone on speaker and asked him to speak. He began by saying to me that my surgery was going to have to be canceled. My CT scan report came back. Not only did they find nodules in one of my lungs but also in both of my lungs. In other words, the cancer had metastasized, and my stage 2 breast cancer was now staged 4. I would have to get to the oncologist immediately.

I laid my head on the table, and I cried as my boss took note of all the pertinent information I would need to know. She held me, and we cried together. She said, "Tina, you gotta be okay. You are strong." I told her I would need to take a couple of days as I walked down the hallway, heading toward my office so that I could get my things and head home. It was the same walk that I had taken for years, but on this day, it felt like the longest walk that I had ever taken. I went back to my desk. Simply put, I couldn't breathe. I couldn't think. I was just stuck and in a daze. My boss asked me if I needed somebody to drive me home. She could see that I was out of it. We both sat there with tears running down our faces. I said, "I'll be okay." I drove home in a fog. I was speechless. When I got home, I went straight to my mom and told her what was going on. She just looked at me, and I think she was in shock too. Knowing her, she did not know what to say because I am sure she didn't want to upset me by asking the wrong questions. I believe I called my sister-in-law next. She was a nurse. Then I called some of my other close family members. I was in disbelief. How could this happen? I was just fine, and now you are telling me I have gone from A to Z in sixty seconds. I had to get myself together.

I began to pray. I said, "Okay, God, I don't know why this happened to me. I don't understand why. All I know, God, is that I need you to hold my hand and walk through this with me. Please don't let me go." I told him, "I don't want to have to go through the vomiting and nausea. I don't want to have diarrhea. I don't want to go through losing my hair. By the way, Lord, even the parts of my hair that won't grow, I need those areas to grow too. Lord, I want people to ask me if I am from Panama or some other country because my hair will be so long and luxurious after all this. I will turn around, flip my hair from my eyes, and say, 'Thank you. I am not from Panama. I am from Oklahoma.' God, all I know is I need you because I am going through this for You and for Your glory. I'm going in, God, knowing that I'm coming out!"

That was the decree that was made. I had my appointment with the oncologist. As did the surgeon, he proceeded to sit down and tell me the details. Here came the medical lingo. What I heard, the revelation that resonated was when he told me that I was going to have to quit my job because he didn't want me to work. He wanted me to go on long-term disability because he said, "We are going to have a long relationship." He said that I had a long journey before me. He proceeded to tell me, "Even if the cancer went away, it could show up again, and it could show up somewhere else in your body." The next thing he said scared the living daylights out of me. He told me he needed me to get another CT scan to make sure the cancer didn't go to my brain. Now at this point, I said, "Okay, God, this is where I am going to draw the line. I cannot have cancer in my brain! I'm doing this for Your glory and for Your glory only. But I cannot have cancer in the brain!" I was unyielding about that, and I was standing my ground.

The CT scan report came back with no cancer having gone to my brain. My doctor was very happy because he said, "We can work with the lungs and breast." He wanted me to take off work the same day though, effective immediately really. That same day that I was in his office, I submitted paperwork for retirement. It was an emotional day because I was going to be leaving my job after twenty-four years. I didn't plan for it to end this way. I had already applied for a long-term disability. Next, I got all the paperwork prepared and ready to start my chemo treatments. Those were going to be scheduled over the course of the next nine weeks. We would see from there. It was dependent upon whether or not the cancer shrinks. Then the doctor would advise me of how much longer I would have to do the treatments.

In the process of getting my insurance together and getting everything processed, my Father had already prepared me for this day, not knowing that this day would even come. I say that because I had taken out two insurance policies when I was married for later down the road, saving for a rainy day, you know, just in case. They both had cancer riders attached to them. I looked into those policies, and little did I know, I had financial blessings sitting right in front of me. I thought I would have to learn how to be content when I thought that my financial foundation had been shattered. With him went his income, and I have a home to pay for. Where there were once two incomes, without what Clifton contributed, I would now have to survive on just mine.

All you have to do is just call on Him. He is able! My mom and my sister are now living with me. I am so grateful to have them right there with me, assisting me while I go through my treatments. I did the math, and it appeared I was still a little short of my goal. So again, I prayed. I said, "God, you know exactly what's going on with my finances. Now I have to retire, and I don't know if I'm going to have enough to make ends meet. God, I'm asking you now to handle my finances. Your will be done. I can't be concerned with how I am going to keep my house and take care of my health. Forgive me, Father, I am going to surrender my finances unto you."

On March 9, 2020, it was my last day at work. My first treatment started the following week. I needed to let go because I chose to trust God. Plus, the doctor said I did not need any stress. So I had no choice but to trust Him. I knew my retirement check was half of my salary. I didn't know where I was going to get the funds from. I told God that I wanted to keep my home because my home is where I found love. My home is where my joy was, where I had peace, and I wanted to keep my home.

My God is awesome! What He will do is always give you a way out. It took me the entire day, but I did call, and I got more information on those cancer policies. I had to find out how they worked. I called on the first one and found out they would be sending me a check in the amount of $10,000 just because of the diagnosis. I called on the next policy, and I had three different policies in one. The first was for a disability that would pay out $1,052 a month. That amount then increased to $3,474 a month since my income would be less now due to retirement. The second part of the policy pays $300 for each chemo treatment, along with $75 for my lab work. I got an additional $50 for the chemotherapy medications. That didn't even include the retirement benefits that started in June.

I also received a call on my birthday in April from the long-term disability office. They told me that I was approved for $2,064 a month, and that would start in October. The delay was okay because I had to wait six months from my first day of leave. In the meantime, I had multiple refunds and unexpected checks that also came in the mail. I am being transparent and giving details not to brag or boast, but to show you that when I turned it over to Him, He blessed me with more than I could have ever imagined. My bank account was pretty much empty. He turned water into wine and allowed me the cushion I needed. No longer did I have to be worried or concerned about my finances. Now I could focus on my health.

I do want to say that I thought I needed Clifton to help me financially. It's like I said, he took his checkbook with him when he left. During all this, it's the year 2020, the year of the pandemic. While God was blessing me financially, we were still enduring the coronavirus. The whole world shut down, and we were ordered to stay home. All businesses had to shut down except for those deemed essential. Clifton was a personal trainer at quite a few of the gyms in our city. When the gym had to close because they are deemed nonessential, it hit his wallet. He subsequently lost a lot of clients. Around that same time, I found a piece of paper that I had tucked away. It said on it, "God, I believe for a financial shift in 2020." I could see between Clifton and I, too, there was a shift. Nevertheless, the blessings were still flowing for me. So much so, I qualified for a brand-new car in an unstable financial environment with no money down. I even got a low-interest rate. The message is God will always take care of His children when we trust Him.

I am saying all this to say that if you trust Him, He is faithful to His Word, and He will supply your needs according to His riches in glory. If you belong to Him and you have that personal relationship with Him and have surrendered all to Him, I am a witness of what God will do. This faith walk is not a game. Sometimes, you are in, and sometimes, you are out. You have to get all the way in and see it before you. You have to see the possibilities before you can have all that is possible. So if you trust Him, do that, just that. That's it, and that's all. I always say either trust Him or turn and walk away. I stand, decree, and declare that I let God know that I don't know how He was going to do it and what He was going to do, but all I knew was that He was going to do something. I held on to His promise to me. What the enemy meant for evil was my diagnosis. I am still walking through this journey, and God is turning it around for my good. He had me prepared for my future. I had no idea what was to come. Tag, I was it! The good news, I have endured twelve chemo treatments. The cancer is shrinking in my breasts and in my lungs. My treatments have been changed to every other week. After three to six months, I will have another CT scan.

Remember when I claimed it, I asked God, and I told him, "I don't want the vomiting, the nausea, or the diarrhea," and so far, today, after sixteen treatments, I haven't had any of these side effects. Now I must say, after my eighth treatment, a side effect called neuropathy has set up in both of my feet. It affects the nerves in your feet, causing them to be numb. I am taking medication, and revisions have been made in my chemo medication to help stop the neuropathy. My coworker bought me a bubble gum pink-colored T-shirt that said, "My God Is Stronger than Breast Cancer!" I wore this shirt every Monday for my sixteenth treatments so far, and I will continue to wear it up until the last treatment. I wear this shirt as a declaration of my faith in God and my healing. Remember when I mentioned not wanting my hair to come out? Needless to say, the chemo medication got me—no long luxurious hair dreams. It was the first week of April, my birth month. I was brushing my hair, and my hair began to shed. I just went and lay down in the bed right then and there. I said, "God, I know I asked you to not allow my hair to come out, along with all the other side effects that I said I did not want. I know, Lord, that this is what goes along with the medication. I see that it is the cause of my hair suddenly shedding." I felt defeated. It was then that I heard His soft, still voice. God said to me, "I would have to remove the old wine before I can give you the new wine." He said,

"I'm going to fulfill my promises. My word is not going to return void. You will get your wavy hair of Panama. I remove the old wine first."

When he told me that, there was a peace that just came over me. I hopped up and went right downstairs to my mom and told her to cut my hair off. I didn't want to have to face it shedding every day. I told her what God said and that I knew he would fulfill His promise to me. I told her to go ahead and cut it all off. I didn't realize how hard it was for her, but she was fighting back the tears. I didn't realize that the entire she was cutting it, she was devastated. I could tell by the way she was chopping it off. I looked in the mirror, and I was like, "What the heck!" It was not like in the movies where it is a beautiful moment, and the camera zooms in with a close-up, highlighting the moment you feel free. She had butchered my hair so bad. I hate to say it, but I would have been better off letting my seven-year-old grandbaby do it. The entire moment was difficult for her. She had to cut off her baby's "golden locks." When my sister got home, I told her, "I need you. Please finish cutting my hair." I wanted her to cut it low, all the way down, as close as she could. She began to cut my hair, and as my hair began to fall on the floor, I said, "I'm gonna be a big girl, and I'm gonna be brave. I'm gonna go and look in the mirror." I looked at myself in the mirror, and I smiled back at myself. Then I said, "It's okay!" God said that His word was not going to return void. He was going to accomplish everything that He said, and I was okay with it all.

To this day, I will not talk to God about how big my problems are. I will talk to my problems about how big my God is. This is my declaration. I will not allow some seasonal, temporary test and/or trial to attack me, trying to make me lose my focus. No weapon formed against me shall prosper. I am not moved by what I see but only by what I believe. I decided to design a journal and a weekly progress worksheet for cancer patients. I did write in my journal daily about my day and recorded on my weekly progress worksheet daily. I decided to create this tool that helped me as a way to help others to journal and log their progress. I want to add scriptures and inspirational sayings on each page, and I for sure want to let them know that they have to have their mindset fixed, that they are "going in, knowing that they are coming out." Regardless of what each day brings, they have to continue to trust and know that God is a healer, Jehovah Rapha, the one that healeth thee.

I placed on my mirror in my bathroom readings I speak every day. It's the best day ever! I also had some declarations that I read every day. I always looked at the positive side of things when it was regarding my health. I was very grateful that my treatment and the subsequent side effects are tolerable. I know they could have been worse. I have always had family and close friend's support. I know that I don't have to worry about anything. They have always been there for me, and I am forever thankful. I had so many people across several states and countries praying and in agreement for my healing and speedy recovery.

Update, after completing sixteen chemo treatments, I had a CT scan that showed no changes in the nodules in my lungs, which is good—meaning the doctor believes that the nodules are not cancerous but still not 100 percent sure that it is not, if you ask me, the reason being for the fact that that chemo did not cause them to shrink, which is a good report. The report did not show anything in the breast. So I had to do another mammogram and ultrasound to make sure of the diagnosis. Those reports showed a decrease in the size of the tumor, but clearly, it had not gone away. It went from 2.1 cm to 1.8 cm.

So now I will have to undergo surgery. I will be having a lumpectomy, and following that, I will be headed to radiation. For now, it may be four to six weeks, five days a week. That may change once I have actually gone through with the surgery. To be honest, I am not excited about it, but I know I have to go through it to get to the other side. So I am good, especially knowing that God is still holding my hand. On the mark, get ready, set, go!

As far as my hair, it has begun to grow back. The color is salt and pepper, more salt than pepper. The texture is straight and silky. It's funny because I've had a few people that wanted to touch it, and some have reached out and touched anyway. Not sure where my hair will go and grow from here. But if you ask me, it may be headed toward Panama. Won't He do it!

My prayer is that all my treatments and the cancer will be completely gone by the time this book is published, in the name of Jesus.

Chapter 16

I'm Shackled in Bondage and I Want to Be Free

I WANT TO share with you that even though I was feeling shackled down and in bondage, God still unlocked the door and allowed me to go free. If you see yourself in any part of my story or if you have found that on your life's journey you have felt like you were shackled, I want you to put the enemy on notice right now!

If the enemy is using your past against you, if he is taking your past hurts and stirring them back up to the surface, dangling your secrets over your head, reminding you about yesterday, he is now on notice! I know how it feels to think back to what was and feel afraid and guilty—thinking if they only knew. You may be feeling right now like the opening of your Pandora's box is only one more lie away, a past truth waiting to be exploited, one unknown truth revealed. It may feel like the door to your deepest past, your dungeon has begun to creep open, so you feel ready to put it all out on the table for everyone to question. You are the best you to tell you about you!

Reveal your truth to you once and for all. It is time to hold your head high, own it, and be healed from it. Bondage is bondage regardless of the many ways it may present itself. Bondage is the condition of not being free because you are strongly influenced by something or someone. What strongly influences you? Who are you influenced by? What is that thing that keeps you from being free? Whisper it to Him right now. He is here for you because He loves you too.

Bondage is when the pain, the anger, the stress, the depression, the hurt from yesterday, your past constantly dangling in your face. If you have never addressed it, how can those old wounds heal? Sometimes, you are too busy to check yourself, admit when you are wrong, or love that person just because God has created them. They, too, have a purpose. What role do they play on your journey? Why are they a part of your story? You are in charge of you. Satan sometimes resurfaces all that pain from yesterday. He triggers you and plucks your strings intentionally, purposefully, vindictively, and dishonestly. He will manipulate you into believing an alternate version when the truth is relative, whether it is in agreement with you or not. You are unable to see other possibilities because of your experiences. You can't fully empathize with all that exists because you can't experience everything that is possible.

You know how a pirate could take a treasure chest and hide it deep below the surface of the earth. It now becomes a buried treasure. It is still filled with precious jewels, artifacts, historically significant and relevant pieces possibly. Treasures are to be treasured. Whatever it is, it's special. The chest is buried though. It's hidden from all to see. It must stay hidden because once the chest is opened, everyone will see what is on the inside. What would be on the inside if your treasure chest opened? There are levels to this too. There are little white lies, infidelities, adultery, dysfunctions, jealously, and abuse, to name a few. You spend a lifetime collecting and condensing, compromising and making do, suppressing what is needed for wholeness. The truth shall set you free. Who can speak about your stuff better than you?

Now imagine pulling a treasure chest up from the ground, having been buried so deep for so long. You will have to get through the dirt and the muck, the layers that have accumulated, in order to get to what is inside. You brush it off, wipe it down, rinse the gross away, whatever it takes to get to the point of it all, the treasure! It is ready now. Are you going to open it?

Here comes the enemy, just as you make the decision that you are ready to be free. Here comes Satan taunting you with this bondage, this old thing that you buried long ago. Now all the pain, the hurt, the anger, and the fear show up, knocking at your door. Sometimes, it interferes with your relationship with your spouse or children. It can definitely interfere with your walk or relationship with God. The enemy wants to trick you. He begins to remind you how worthless you are, how sinful you were. He will even have the audacity to try keeping you from praising God "with all that sin and mess in your life."

For some reason, even though we know better, we still believe and take heed to what the enemy wants to tell us. We have to always know who we are though. Remember what God has said, "For all have sinned, and come short of the glory of God" (Romans 3:23). He also said, "When we accept Him, all unrighteousness is forgiven" (1 John 1:9). If we confess our sins, He is faithful and just to forgive us our sins and to cleanse us from all unrighteousness. For He is faithful and just to forgive us of all, not some one-half or one-fourth or even five-eight, but all our unrighteousness. And by the way, He forgives us for our sins when we ask for forgiveness.

First, call that thing out, whatever it is:

- Rape
- Molestation
- Incest
- Alcohol
- Drugs
- Physical abuse
- Mental abuse
- Child abuse
- Being abandoned as a child
- Suicide attempt
- Abortion
- Adultery
- Victims of teenage pregnancy
- Divorced

- Child caught in the middle of a divorce, who do you choose?
- Fear
- Homosexuality
- Low self-esteem
- Hatred
- Jealousy and envy
- Lying
- Unforgiveness
- Soul ties

There are many, many more, but this is enough to at least scratch the surface, triggering what has been buried. If you are being held captive by any of these or other things, ask God to help you. Let your Father know that you want to be delivered, and He will set you free right now. Let Him know that you want the strongholds that the enemy is using against you removed. The enemy may be trying to hinder and stagnate you. He may be trying to keep you from moving forward. Let the enemy know you are covered by the blood of Jesus, and the assignment of the enemy has been canceled and nullified! The enemy will constantly try to bring your past up to taunt you with it continuously. He likely won't give up without a fight. That's his job. That is why you must pray without ceasing. That is why you must communicate with your Father daily about everything. Pray for strength and wisdom so that you may endure whatever is to come.

We have to release the layers of pain that we are holding on to. As hard as it may be to forgive them, do it. Then forgive yourself. Now let it go for real. You can't memorialize a slate that has been wiped clean. Don't keep rehearsing the pain either. Stop talking about it and giving it life. Pain does not fall out on its own. It has to be released. You have to get to a place before the throne of God where you humble yourself. Be transparent even to yourself. It happened, but let the enemy know that his reign is over. He is no longer the master of your thoughts, emotions, or actions. You are in charge of you. Boldly speak over your life. Let the enemy know that God will and shall deliver you from being captive.

When you call out to the Lord, surrender unto him. Let him know that you need him to help you get through the darkness and the pain. You want to give him everything that is you. Don't be afraid to ask Him to lead you and order your steps. You are a vessel unto him. In 2 Corinthians 10:3–5, it says, "For though we walk in the flesh, we do not war according to the flesh. For the weapons of our warfare are not carnal but mighty in God for pulling down strongholds, casting down arguments and every high thing that exalts itself against the knowledge of God, bringing every thought into captivity to the obedience of Christ."

You can cry out to Him because He loves you and wants nothing but the best for you. If He did it for me, He would do it for you. "For there is no respect of persons with God," says Roman 2:11. He loves you just as much as He loves me. He wants you to be free so that you can totally walk in the purpose, the plan, and the destiny that He has already prepared for you. You have to trust and know that if you call upon Him, He will answer thee. Why? Because He loves you just that much.

Here's a saying I want to leave with you, "You can be incarcerated, but you don't have to become institutionalized." You are in charge of you. The only time you can learn strength is when first you are weak. The only time you can respect the victory is when you have first known defeat. That's when you find out who you are and who you're not. Through your failures, you will learn to trust Him. Through your setbacks, you can have comebacks. Through your storms, you can see and have peace. Through your suffering, you can see His glory manifested. Remember, God will never give you more than you can bear. He would not have allowed you to go through the valley if He didn't know that you already have in you the ability to go through it. Your success is His glory. He is your Father. "For I know the plans I have for you," declares the Lord. "Plans to prosper you and not to harm you, plans to give you hope and a future," says Jeremiah 29:11. God has been bragging on your ability to get through it. You are His creation. He knows when you depend on Him. Once you come through to the other side, you will see him manifested. I'll tell you there is nothing like being set free from bondage and finding yourself resting in God's arms.

My prayer for you:

Father, we just praise you. We honor and adore you. We lift your holy name and thank you for who you are.

We come in your mighty name Lord, through your resurrecting power. You said in your Word, Lord, that we could come boldly to the throne of grace to obtain mercy in the time of need. So here we are, Lord.

Father, we thank you in advance for removing the shackles and loosening the chains so that my sister or brother can be free from the snares of the enemy.

I decree and declare that the blood of Jesus has removed and washed away any sins that have been committed. I pray You keep them strengthened God and remind them that they are more than conquerors. Remove the residue of the scars and the memories that continue to taunt them. Right now! Lord, we claim the victory that the chains are broken.

Satan! I serve you notice on this day. I decree and declare that you no longer have dominion nor authority over this vessel. This vessel, in the name of Jesus, belongs to God.

Satan! You must let go of their mind, their emotions, and "Lord! I pray Your will be done!" in the name of Jesus. Right now, in the name of

Jesus, I declare you are strong with the strength to break free. Your burden has been lifted, and victory is yours.

Father, I thank you for releasing the pain that has been suppressed and hiding while blocking the release of restoration and recovery. Father, I ask that you release them from being held prisoner and release those held captive to their past pain. Release them to move forward and allow the past to be uprooted, removing all the shame and guilt.

Father, I pray and agree that they will be able to let go of every traumatic experience, and they will allow your presence, your peace, and your love to be received. Father, I thank you for keeping them even when they could not keep themselves. I thank you for the peace that surpasses all understanding and for guarding their hearts and their mind. I thank you for restoring their joy and removing anything from their past that will block and hinder them from being released from the cloud of darkness.

Lord, I pray for their freedom, and in a matter of seconds, Holy Spirit, I ask that you block out every memory that still resides and immediately purge any residue of their past. Father, we thank you that there is no burden that we carry that is too heavy to be placed at your feet. Father, I pray that you teach them how to forgive themselves for holding themselves hostage because of their past.

I thank you, Lord, in advance, for what you are going to do and how you are going to set this vessel free from bondage, free from being shackled, and free from the mental chains holding them. Father, I thank you for the Word that reminds them that greater is He (who is God) that is in you than he (the enemy) that is in the world.

Thank you, Lord, for the plan that you have already said is so and in place for their lives even when they were yet in their mother's womb. I thank you, Father, for their freedom and the liberty to walk in the path that you have already ordained. In the precious and mighty name of Jesus, I pray. Amen!

Now walk in your freedom and say goodbye to yesterday. Celebrate your today while looking forward to cherishing your tomorrow. You've got this!

About the Author

TINA ANDREA PULLUM was born in Oklahoma City, Oklahoma. She is the oldest of five children. She received a degree in interior design from the Fashion Institute of Design and Merchandise. She has traveled around the world and back. Tina, along with her mother, are the creators of the Heart of a Woman Celebration for over one thousand women across seven years.

She is the founder of several workshops: Learning to Love Yourself Even the More (developed for the men and women participants of The Valley Oasis Domestic Violence Shelter), the Princess Masterpiece (for young girls in Kenya and Africa), and Who's Loving You (for the Living Praise Christian Center where she is a member and works faithfully in the ministry).

Tina has two children and two grandchildren. They are why her heart beats. She lives by the motto, "You only live once, but if you do it right, once is enough." Tina likes to leave a little sparkle wherever she goes. She doesn't just dream her life. She lives her dreams. This is her first book.

CPSIA information can be obtained
at www.ICGtesting.com
Printed in the USA
FSHW011550090821
83762FS